Travel Secrets

Insider guide to planning, affording, and taking more vacations!

Second Edition

Anita Kaltenbaugh

Copyright © 2017 Anita Kaltenbaugh

2nd edition Copyright © 2017

All rights reserved. This book, or any portion thereof, may not be reproduced in any form without permission.

Printed in the United States of America

ISBN:1461028329
ISBN-13:9781461028321

All my love and thanks to William Clark's great-great-grandson for helping me see the world.

CONTENTS

Introduction ... i

1. **What Is This Book?** What it can do for you and how it can change your life. ... 1

2. **Why Travel?** If you are asking that question, this chapter is calling your name. ... 15

3. **Where To?** Choices--east, west, north, south--the possibilities are endless. ... 25

4. **When is the Best Time to Travel?** The correct answer would be anytime is a good time for vacation. Planning with some flexibility, however, can assist in saving $$$ and adding enjoyment. ... 33

5. **How Do I Afford It?** Money is the one travel necessity we should take with us (at least, a little bit). Whether it is Hamilton, Jackson, Grant or Franklin, here's the inside information on making those old men work for less. ... 41

6. **99 Secrets That Will Change the Way You Travel and Save You Money** - A list of travel tips and secrets to help you pay for this book 99 times over. ... 50

7. **Top Hottest Websites and Smartphone Travel Apps to Save You Money** - Check out these hot travel apps/websites before you give your credit card number for another hotel room, airplane ticket or travel package. ... 69

8. **Secrets to Making Your Next Vacation a Trip of a Lifetime** - All vacations can be trips of a lifetime— a little planning and research will make every trip its own unique memory. ... 83

9. **10 Ways to Go Green, and Save Enough Money for a Vacation** (Yes, it's true.) Follow these simple going-green suggestions and in one year help save the planet *and* save enough money for a vacation. ... 87

10. **10 Vacation Ideas and Trips, All for a Tank of Gas**...Who says you have to spend a lot of cash to take a vacation? Pack a lunch, jump in the car and take a vacation for the cost of a tank of gas. ... 96

One lifetime, so many trips, get started now!

Introduction

Travel Secrets are Everywhere

I can spend hours looking up amazing photographs on vacation destination websites, dreaming about an exotic journey to Nepal, discovering a paradise island hidden deep in the South Pacific, or wandering the winding, narrow cobblestone streets of Prague. It consumes and excites me and makes me want to get up and go.

Traveling to every continent in this lifetime is a bucket list goal for me. Putting my foot down on the ground in every continent on this earth would fulfill a lifelong dream. Seeing something new in the world, escaping out of the box of today's society, and giving responsibility a rest for a weekend, a week, or ten days is the greatest medicine I can imagine and it doesn't come in a pharmacy prescription bottle.

It's the second decade of the millennium. We are so lucky to have travel at our fingertips, and I do mean at our fingertips. It's available 24 hours a day, on a smartphone or on the newest tablet - even on your smart TV. Flat screen monitors can take you where you want to go digitally, in high definition (HD) or UHD, in seconds. We can see our desired destinations just by googling them.

With so many choices available to us and so many offers on the internet, on television, and in magazines, *travel secrets are everywhere*! You just need to know how to discover them before spending all your time and money.

This is a book about *travel secrets.* Secrets to enrich your life ... Secrets that will get you up off the couch and traveling more. Secrets that will save you money so you can afford to make travel part of your everyday life. We need to understand these secrets so we can sort through the overwhelming plethora of travel information out there and save the time spent looking up the wrong information.

We live in a remarkable era of technology – amazing hi-tech automation is being developed every day. Remember *The Jetsons*? Watch the cartoon again and see what real technology exists now, that was once just a futuristic gimmick in a cartoon.

This constantly changing technology offers so many unbelievable possibilities of seeing the world. Today's technology is truly mind-blowing! Magically, it continues to be incessantly created and upgraded, making travel easier than it has ever been during mankind's existence.

Stop and think for a minute. Can you imagine how monumental and magical travel would seem to our ancestors? It would change lives, nations, and worlds. Do we understand this gift of travel and possibilities that we have available to us in today's world? It's hard to comprehend. Perhaps we should take a glance over our shoulders and look back in time for a moment to grasp the travel advantages we have today. If we know how hard it was for those who journeyed before us. it might inspire us to take advantage of how much easier travel is today.

Back when travel was difficult and hard to arrange, it must have been a tedious task to organize any kind of travel. Getting from Point A to Point B wasn't just a push of a button or a phone call, or giving a 16-digit credit card to Expedia. It was dangerous, exciting and uncertain, difficult, and unknown.

Luxury accommodations, rooms with a view, room service, or getting an aisle seat were not high on the list. The reality involved hoping you had enough coins or bartering valuables to pay for your fare; not whether you'd printed out your electronic boarding pass 24 hours before and were in Group B. Choices and preferences were nonexistent; you hoped for any vessel or way of transportation available.

Travel needs of the past consisted of having enough food and water for you and your horses and a spare wagon wheel for your covered wagon. Most definitely at the top of the list of travel necessities would be a weapon to protect you on the journey. There was no airport metal detectors or security screening, back then. Yes, most travel was done on a need-to-travel basis. Imagine the limitations. Over a century ago you hoped and prayed you would make it through bad weather, sickness, plagues, and pirates.

In the 1800s, your hotel accommodations consisted of the first candle in the window that you stumbled upon. With any luck and with a knock on a door, the local farmer might put you up in the barn, or perhaps you'd find a shelter where travelers slept three or four to a bed with strangers. It was not usually the custom to say no to a weary traveler with no place to lay their head. Travelers were put up for the night out of human dignity.

There were no advertisements for 400-thread-count Egyptian cotton sheets or heavenly beds with I-pod docks advertised here. No, it was a sleeping area made of straw on the ground with some type of shelter over your head.

No one back then could fathom what it would be like to travel thousands of miles in a lifetime; just as we find it hard to imagine what it would be like to only travel 50 miles in a lifetime, when now we can travel 5000 miles in a day.

How many miles have you traveled in your life? Think about it for a moment. It's very difficult to compute, especially if you traveled for your job. It may surprise you to learn just how large the number is. Today, we have a travel app for that. Airlines will also compute your miles and reward you for being part of the "million miles club".

Everything's faster in today's world. Depending on where you are traveling to or from, travel is lightning quick - at least, compared to history. It takes minutes or just a few hours, and certainly less than 24 hours, to go around the world. In 6 hours and 20 minutes you can fly from New York City to London, England. Yes, in less than a typical day at the office you can travel to another continent in a comfortable mode of transportation.

In the 1800s it would take an entire day to travel 70 miles, and now we fly 70 miles in less than 10 minutes. In less than 5 hours you can fly from Los Angeles to New York. Coast to coast in less than 5 hours? Imagine what the pioneers would have thought of a five-hour trip across the United States of America? Mind boggling. Astonishing. Unthinkable. Would they have believed us?

Today, all the constraints our ancestors witnessed have vanished. With the explosion of technology, traveling is so fast that most people are not aware of the latest and greatest secrets when it comes to traveling, planning vacations, and costs. I understand, because it's hard to keep up with all the changes.

The travel suggestions in this book can save thousands of dollars for just one adventure - tips that can mean staying in a luxury room versus a below-standard motel room - *at the same rate.*

Employing these insights allowed me to travel more often than I'd ever imagined doing. It allowed me to save money for future trips so I could take more of them and experience luxury vacations instead of budget trips. Using these secrets, my husband and I have managed to take over 99 vacations in three years.

Ninety-nine vacations?

Sounds impossible, when you say it. It's not impossible at all. There are 365 days and 52 weekends in a year. Even if you are short on time off, you can still take weekend getaways. Does that count as a vacation? Of course it does. The definition of a <u>vacation,</u> according to the Encarta Dictionary, is as follows: "vacation: a break from work – a period of time devoted to rest, travel, or recreation."

The definition of <u>travel</u> in the Encarta dictionary is "the activity of going on journeys, usually using a form of transportation, or visiting different places." So yes, by all definitions a weekend trip (a break from work for recreation and visiting someplace else) is definitely a vacation.

You might think that 99 vacations in three years must have cost a fortune. No, I'm not a trust fund baby, a celebrity, or multi-billionaire. Like my coal miner, steel worker father from Western Pennsylvania who played the lottery week after week, we have not won the lottery even occasionally; but we have made it our goal in life to touch every continent.

Travel is like winning another type of lottery - the lottery of travel and adventure, meeting people from different villages and walks of life, and understanding this vast world, which at times seems so large yet in other moments, so very small, with closed borders. Technology brings the world closer than ever before. Our borders are shrinking because of our *Jetson*-like devices.

Perspective and an appreciation for others comes out of travel. Having a good travel partner is not a necessity, but if you do happen to find one who shares the love of travel and adventure, it can work out to be a huge plus and can save money. Sometimes two can travel more cheaply than one.

My partner of choice happens to have a unique history of travel and adventure, since his great-great-grandfather is William Clark of the historical explorers Lewis and Clark. It is hard to imagine what Lewis and Clark, such great map creators and adventure travelers, would think of MapQuest or a GPS app on your smartphone. Let's not forget Sacagawea. History shows that without this Native American woman, Lewis and Clark might have been lost, tortured, or possibly killed. She helped guide and translate and stood as a symbol of peace for the explorers. I wonder what they would make of all this travel technology? Regardless of what technology you have when you travel, I'm sure they would agree it takes planning, collaboration, and a good traveling partner or partners to make it all work.

So, as I write down my travel secrets with my husband, the great-great-grandson of Clark, it appears the apple does not fall far from the tree. My husband being Clark's descendant has had an impact on my adventurous spirit. He has a passion for traveling and exploring the world and sharing the millions of unique and incredible experiences this planet has to offer with everyone else. He doesn't have to draw a map or chart rivers, as his ancestors did across unknown territory, but perhaps he has me, his pseudo-Sacagawea, to chart different pathways and help others get from here to there.

Thank you to my husband's great-great-grandfather, William Clark, and to all the historic men and women who created the ability and the desire to travel and explore the world when it wasn't easy.

We are spoiled when it comes to the ease of transportation in the 21st century. The barriers of our ancestors are gone, and now the barriers only exist in our minds. We create barriers to travel and vacation by not making time, not saving money, and not planning. Let this book help you with all three areas. Buy this book for the friend, relative or boss who needs to take a vacation.

Learn how to plan more vacations. Make time to get away with loved ones, or try new adventures on your own. Whether you travel close or go far, it can change your world. Learn how to "go green" in your home and save enough money this year for a vacation. Help the planet and earn a vacation! Shame on us if we don't take advantage of what we have at our fingertips. Go ahead: decide you want to travel, take more vacations, get away for the weekend, and plan to see the world.

What's the worst that can happen? ...Oh yes, you finally take a vacation and create memories to last a lifetime.

"The world is a book and those who do not travel read only one page." – St. Augustine

Chapter 1

What is this book? *What it can do for you and how it can change your life*

Romantic cottages on a private beach, century-old castles in the Alps, and tree houses in the subtropical rainforest of Belize all paint amazing pictures in our minds. Words cannot describe the scenery that exists in this magical world of ours. Everywhere you explore, you will find charming villages, ancient civilizations, and new technological cities. The unique faces of native people will come with their stories of mysterious homelands and inspire your mind. A journey full of adventure and the excitement of the unknown is waiting for you. Travel, take action, and make a passage into something new. The memories of your travel days will stay with you forever. They are priceless.

This book can help you understand the world of travel. It will clarify why you should be traveling and it will provide simple insights on the travel industry that are easy to find, use, and save you money on your vacations.

How to use this book is up to you. Yes, you can skip around and read the chapters that will immediately help you save money for vacation, or you can read it from the beginning. My suggestion is: start from the beginning. Better yet, go to the dollar store, buy a notebook, title it in big bold letters, TRAVEL, and as you read this, get organized and take notes (you'll thank me later). Compiling all your thoughts and ideas in one place, listing apps you want to download, and writing ideas as they come to you will be worth the time. There are no rules-- but organizing and having notes in one place (either online or by hand) will assist in your future travel success.

If you stood in Times Square and asked random strangers "Do you like to take vacations?", what do you think the answer would be? Well, unfortunately, anytime you stop and ask folks a question in the middle of the street, they might think you are trying to sell something and most likely will be afraid to strike up a conversation. If they were honest, however, who wouldn't answer *yes*? Perhaps you'd get a few responses of "Yes, I love to take vacations, but who has the time?" or "Yes, I love vacations, but I don't have the money." And a few "Yes, I go every chance I can - I'm on vacation now!"

People love vacationing. Smiles and wonderment light up children's faces at Disney World, at the beach, even on a picnic. Adults look relaxed and worry-free whether they're on a tropical island, reading a good book in a hammock, or gazing in awe at the Eiffel Tower.

Vacations are wonderful mini-adventures in your book of life. They add spice to the daily grind, take you out of the box you're living in, and help you ease out of your comfort zone of daily routines. There's no mistaking it – vacations make you feel good.

What adds to an outstanding trip besides the adventure, food, and memories, however, is the knowledge that you got a great deal. If you know your cost is about half the price of others who may be on the same trip, you'll get an extra benefit from vacation, besides the journey. Knowing the secrets to the travel industry and how to get the best bang for your buck is enlightening and invigorating. Believe me – it makes an incredible and enjoyable trip even more wonderful.

Let's be clear – I'm not talking about being cheap. Actually, the words "cheap" or "frugal" don't quite describe the act of getting the best deals. Words like "smart", "knowledgeable", and "flexible" sound more accurate. It's all about travel economics. Personally, I am particular about where I stay, what type of amenities are available, and accommodations offered; and the luxury factor is always at the top of the list. I just want to obtain the best deal for the lowest price.

The way I see it, I'm on vacation - and who doesn't want to feel comfortable and luxurious lying in bed a little longer than usual on your coveted time off? Typically, it is on vacation when you make up for lost time at home; paying more attention to your significant other because you finally have the time to do so. Vacation is an escape from the routine of home and work.

Yes, there will be vacation days when you are constantly on the go, exploring all day long and only using your room to sleep at night on sunny days full of sunshine and deep blue water clear as a mirror, with colorful parrot fish circling around. Or on adventure vacations of hiking and camping, where tents and outdoor fresh air are part of the experience. Coupled with those adventure days, however, will (hopefully) be a few relaxation days. If not, you should try it. You may find it adds immense pleasure to your vacation. It should resemble anything but your daily routine, with no alarms savagely going off in the dark morning, no having to get up to walk the dog, feed the kids or even rush to beat the traffic to work. It is a time to lounge, breathe, and take care of *you* before starting out on whatever adventure comes your way. Please note: with an attitude like this, adventure and leisure will chase you.

So, it only makes sense that when you are on vacation, you should have more time for respite; so if you're not used to doing this on trips, plan it into your busy schedule. The point is: if you're relaxing, why shouldn't it be on 300-thread-count sheets with great lighting and room service at your beck and call? Since you will be spending more time on the bed or in the bed than you normally would at home, you should enjoy the atmosphere and not settle for dirty, cheap, non-luxurious hotel or motel rooms with uncomfortable beds.

Money. Luxury costs, and you would rather not spend it on a room. Right? It's a valid argument; but what if I can show you the secrets to paying the same costs for your luxury hotel room as the cheap motel inn down the road? Why not?

Being cheap is not the point of this book. Being smart and knowing a few tricks and secrets is the motive. Paying 30% to 50% off the regular room rate just makes you smarter than the average bear. I like to be smarter than the average bear... it makes me feel good.

Men and women sweat out the 40+ hour work week so they can support their families and enjoy simple pleasures in life. In today's economic times, money is tight, and planning a vacation to a mysterious, exciting destination can seem like a luxury far off in the distance.

Yes, we all cut out that photo of the palm tree dangling over a pristine white beach with clear blue water and a hammock swaying in the wind, or the snow-covered mountain with a log cabin nestled in a forest with a stream running in front and the snowy peaks reflected in a lake. We picture ourselves lying comfortably on the warm, baby-powder-white sand with turquoise clear water in the background, or stretched out on a bear skin rug in front of a cozy fireplace, gazing at a snow-capped forest one we just skied down, flying at high speed, trailblazing through fresh snow. Whatever your ideal image is, or your picture-perfect postcard, why not make it a reality?

I guarantee that 90% of the folks with a bulletin board in front of them at work have some type of picture of a vacation or a screen saver of a fantastic, far-away location on their computer - a scenic spot that instantly transports them away to a dream location they would love to escape to. Is it a deep red sun setting over an island on the ocean? Powdered snow trails with glistening treetops and fresh fallen snow? Or an old memory of a good beach trip from the past, or a city sparkling with energy and hot night spots? It could be motorcycle riding in the Arizona desert, exploring medieval European cities by foot on cobblestone trails, or scuba diving the Blue Hole in Belize. Any of these could be your postcard.

For years, my postcard was a ripped-out magazine ad of a private island in the Florida Keys with blue, blue water, a clapboard cottage built on stilts over the mesmerizing sea, and a wooden plank runway to get to the deck. The entire island was available for rent, including an amazing house, private boat, and clothing-optional beach. (It's your island, right?)

Somewhere, we all have that photograph, even if it's in our minds. You know the one I'm referring to. It's there: a place to escape to, a place to relax in, and a place to yearn for. Our bucket list of travel. If you don't know it consciously, you know it subconsciously.

We imagine life is better in that place on the postcard. No worries, no work, and no schedules. We envision the movie that we already created, and we are in the starring role. When we watch the movie in our mind, our character is relaxed, or ecstatically joyful, or full of adrenaline. Our beautiful postcard snapshot is a magical land where everything is better. More romance, more living, more laughter.

Well, dreams can become reality. Just the mere fact that you are reading this book puts you above the average population. Most folks think about traveling the world and taking more vacations, but don't know how they can accomplish or even afford it. Guess what? You are not in the typical group of vacation planners. You are researching a better way to travel and spend less money just by reading this book. Anything worthwhile in life takes a little work-- so, congratulations for putting in the effort.

Okay, let's go back to your dream postcard. Picture it in your mind. Close your eyes. Can you see it? Perhaps you have a few of them, and can't decide between them. Perfect: it's okay to have many dream postcards. In fact, if you are reading this book, I guarantee you have several images flashing through your mind. If not, by the time you are done, you will.

Let me ask you a few questions. Answer them honestly.

Do you think it would change your life to use free time exploring other places and get away from the everyday routine? Switch it up. Relax on the routine.

Would it be beneficial to spend quality time with yourself, with a significant other, or with family members in a relaxed atmosphere, in a new destination?

Would it add a little spice to your life to learn about others and step out of the box?

I hoped you answered yes.

New adventures, opening your mind, trying new things, meeting new people, traveling with others, and understanding the world can only help expand your mind, your heart, and your soul. Change and adventure can change your life.

It is a fact that those who stop trying new things tend to stay in the same routine. Those people who are afraid of change and who have a fear of different experiences grow older faster, are sick more often, and have a lesser quality of life. (I'm not making this up).

Stress does terrible things to our immune system, cardiovascular system, and overall health. Depression, anxiety, obesity, and heart attacks all may be caused by stress. John De Graff, documentary filmmaker and author of *Take Back Your Time*, is an advocate for vacation and recreation time for Americans. There is even a public policy agenda advocating for mandatory vacation time. Facts exist that prove relaxation and leisure time are part of overall good health. The lack of them can lead to serious consequences. The statistical information is readily available: you can find it online, ask your physician, or watch a Discovery Channel documentary. Knowing that vacation improves your health is a fact; so what is stopping you from taking care of yourself and taking more vacations?

Money, Money, Money. Okay, I know most of you believe that more vacations equal less stress. You agree that taking a vacation may change your life, improve your health, and add adventure and happiness, but the first thing that pops in your mind is MONEY.

Where do you get the money? I know what you're thinking. In today's economy, vacations cost too much, are difficult to plan, and will use up all those personal funds and time that you are saving for a rainy day.

Well, the problem with saving time for a rainy day is that in the meantime, you miss all the sunshine days, while you are waiting for it to rain. You can put things on hold, but life won't wait for you.

Sure, it is smart to save a few vacation or personal days for emergencies you can't predict, but it is smarter to use your vacation time to enrich your life and enjoy it for the real reason you earn vacation time in the first place: to go on VACATION!!!

Many people are savers. I admit that I have been a saver all my life. Saving money, yes; but saving pleasures - no. What does it mean to be a saver? Well, if you have a shirt or dress or something new that you have put away for a special occasion, and it is still hanging in your closet with the tags on, you are showing signs of being a saver.

I know we have all heard the stories of the woman or man who saved the good china, the sexy nightgown, or the money under the mattress for just the right moment. The story goes: when the saver passes away, their family finds all the saved items - the unworn nightgown, new china and the rainy day money - so they bury them in the saved nightgown or saved outfit, with the good china. The money, all divided up by the remaining relatives, doesn't amount to much; but it sure would have financed a great vacation for the person who died, or paid for several trips of a lifetime.

We all know the saying, "You can't take it with you," regardless of what "it" is. We also all know that life goes by pretty darn fast. Usually, when you realize how fast life goes by and truly believe that saying, most of it has passed you by.

Hopefully, we can learn from the wisdom of others.

Time and time again we watch the movie or read an article about a terminal patient; the sad story of the young ambitious woman who learns she has cancer, or the middle-aged workaholic who is told he has six months left to live. What do they all do? You know the story - different characters, different dreams, different bucket lists. They live life. The truth of the matter is: they finally get what life is all about.

Why? Because it's staring them in the face. It's a wakeup call they wished they'd had earlier, before time was a rare thing. Faced with the reality that time is running out, they want to live it up, travel the world, be kind to others, and "talk sweeter, love deeper" as Tim McGraw croons in the old classic "Live Like You Were Dying."

So, running out of time makes you want to enjoy it and take the time. What a terrible Catch-22. When you finally realize it is not about money or hours spent at work, but making memories, helping others, and learning about the world, it may be because you only have limited time left.

Tick tock, tick tock - the clock's hands are moving faster.

What do you do if you don't want to become a Lifetime movie, or another story about "could have, should have, and would have"? Oh, I have an idea: couldn't we learn from those before us, who have been told they have a terminal illness? Listen and respect their position when they tell us to live each day as if it were our last? Don't you think there's value to the advice given by those who know they are short on time?

So, for a moment, throw away the cost and time excuses. We can all find time for the things we know are good for us. It's amazing, but true. We will take time for preventive dentist or doctor appointments, on schedule, every six months. We get our teeth cleaned, get a check-up, pay money for our health and even life insurance every month, but where is the plan for preventive care through good life moments. Vacation insurance? Why not?

No one looks forward to these preventive expensive items; but yes, they are important. So why not add a preventive health measure that you can look forward to? When is the last time you heard someone talk excitedly about their dentist or doctor appointment, or uploaded pictures and told stories about their visit on Facebook? Never. It doesn't happen. We know vacations are good for you; however, doctors recommend them to prevent stress, nervous breakdowns, and create balance. How about adding vacations into your preventive appointments? You don't start cleaning your teeth after they are decayed; you do it on a routine basis to take care of them. Don't wait to take vacations until you retire: make them part of your preventive care.

Taking vacations as a preventive measure will pay off just like the health physicals and teeth cleaning. You will enjoy your life as you are living it, be in the moment, and not just think about the moments you should have experienced when it is too late. The benefits of vacations are endless, for your future and your overall health.

Knowing where to look, where to go, and how to fit taking vacations into your life is the first step.

So not only is this a book about how to save money on traveling; but it's about how to change your life and live longer. Maybe traveling is like finding the fountain of youth. It is an adventure that is sure to bring back your youth and childlike ways, helping you remember old times, feel younger, and create new memories. So take ten minutes out of your day right now and answer the questions on the next page, to get started on your journey.

These questions will help you plan your future journeys (yes, get out a piece of paper and write these down - trust me, it will be worth it). Better yet: I repeat my earlier advice: go to the dollar store, buy one of those little notebooks for $1, and start your travel journal.

1. We all have our vacation postcards, either physically hanging up or tucked away mentally. What is the first postcard that comes into your mind?

_____

2. If you won a contest and could pick a free vacation to a destination of your choice, where would it be?

Okay, this one might be tough, list your top three.

1.

2.

3.

_____

How much do you think it would cost you to go on any of the above vacations to the destination of your choice?

_____

3. Make a bucket list of ten places you would like to see before you die. Don't worry: this may change. Start with the first ten places that come to mind. If you can't narrow it down and you have twenty-five places or a hundred, write them all down. Make your travel bucket list.

1. _____

2. _____

3. _____

4. _____

5. _____

6. _____

7. _____

8. _____

9. _____

10. _____

"Twenty years from now you will be more disappointed by the things you didn't do than by the ones you did do. So throw off the bowlines, sail away from the safe harbor. Catch the trade winds in your sails. Explore. Dream. Discover."- Mark Twain.

Chapter 2

Why travel? Why travel, really? *If you are asking that question this chapter is calling your name*

Why travel? To me, that is like asking the question, why breathe? Seriously, traveling is the essence of our existence. It doesn't matter if your vacations are near or far, as long as you travel. This means leaving the space you reside in and exiting your current routine to physically take a trip to somewhere new, revisiting a landmark or exploring a place of your youth.

Imagine if our ancestors decided that it was too much of a hassle to travel. You know – didn't want the bother of taking a trip because of a few travel obstacles. You think **you** have travel obstacles? Imagine your ancestors' travel to-do list for a trip. Let's just put this in perspective one more time, so you realize how easy we have it today.

1. Build covered wagon.

2. Hand carve new wooden wheels.

3. Grow or hunt food in order to pack nourishment for the journey.

4. Pack feed and water for horses.

5. Pack enough survival necessities, blankets, weapons, and clothing to endure a long journey.

6. Map a safe travel route without pirates, bandits or thieves, since all the money for the trip is with you. Bring enough money or items to barter for the duration of the journey. (No credit card or travel checks in case you get robbed.)

7. Estimate length of journey with unforeseen weather conditions.

8. Complete a will or "in case of" instructions for any property, livestock or children left behind. (It was not uncommon for the return trip to never materialize, due to unforeseen conditions).

9. Quit your employment or work out a deal upon your return (saying a prayer that your job will still be available). In the past, a trip took extensive travel time and vacation time was rare or nonexistent.

Of course, the list of essential travel items that didn't exist back then are countless:

No cell phones to call for help, no 7-11's, Circle Ks or convenience stores to pick up supplies or any necessary forgotten trip item. No fast food drive thru to grab a bite to eat while on the road. No travel maps. No internet. No texting. No Wi-Fi. No car radio. No road signs. No public transportation. No covered wagon or wooden wheel fix-it repair shops. The list is endless.

They couldn't use Google Maps to plot their journey, and had no freeways, train stations or airports. No weather channel, and no weather app on their smartphone or five-day weather forecaster on television. No travel apps to pre-book their hotels. And, yes, not even a Starbucks to keep you awake.

Yes, there were more obstacles than we could ever fathom.

Today's modern travel conveniences are taken for granted.

Let's think about it for a little longer.

Picture this: you just need to get away and take some time off from the daily grind. Winter is coming soon, and after a hard summer of plowing the field, hunting the meat for the winter, and suffering through the humidity, you need a vacation. The closest beach is approximately 600 miles away. Your perception of a 600-mile journey is limited because in your lifetime, very few have actually traveled 600 miles.

Sure, you have seen faraway lands in a picture book, and a black and white photo of an ocean, and you think to yourself, *does this really exist*? Is there really a larger body of water bigger than Farmer Miller's pond where you swam since childhood? Where do you sleep and find supplies?

Imagine the planning that would be involved in taking a simple beach vacation, 100 years ago.

Sounds difficult and nearly impossible. Yet, many still traveled. They ventured east, west, north, and south with their families and their animals. They crossed jagged, teetering high mountain ranges and wild, rapidly flowing rivers enveloped in varying climates.

Enough about the past, right? Why belabor the point, right?

Wrong. *This* is why you should travel more right now--- isn't the answer obvious?

Because we can.

It's all about ease and accessibility. Technology allows everyone to become their own travel agent. Resources are available that can make a salmon fisherman in Alaska an expert on the best white beaches of St. Lucia.

In today's internet world, we have power. From 3000 miles away we can take a virtual tour and see the exact room we are going to stay in on our vacation. We can zoom in on the white down comforter with a brown stripe around its edge. We can focus on the glistening marble flooring, the floor to ceiling windows looking over the city of our choice, and the 42-inch flat plasma TV; all from our phone.

Does that astonish you? In less than a minute on the internet, you can check the weather for your holiday vacation, see your hotel on a map with nearby restaurants, and even order groceries to be delivered to your room before you arrive.

Is it magic to be able to click on the photo of the bed you are going to sleep in halfway around the world? Our ancestors would believe it is witchcraft.

Technology today would be "the unexplained," to travelers of the past. They would think we were time travelers.

Today we have incredible advantages that make travel easier than ever before. It wasn't until the Microsoft Corporation launched Expedia as part of Microsoft Network in October 1996 that online travel for consumers was even a concept.

Expedia was the first online travel service to be offered by a major company such as Microsoft. Many have since followed in its path, making the choices of travel sites somewhat confusing to new travel planners. Historically, the typical train of thought was: consumers are too busy to plan their own plane reservations, hotel reservation, and car rental. Many travel agents thought the idea of a site like Expedia would certainly assist travel agents, but not consumers.

People initially joined the travel industry because of their love of travel and adventure, never imagining that at a click of a button today, anyone can book flights, plan the length of time between plane changes, or create exotic, unique itineraries of European cities in ten days. Who could imagine having the ability to watch real-time web cams of snow falling on a ski slope at ten thousand foot elevations - the very same ski slope that you would ski the next morning, five thousand miles away from your house? Oh, yeah: you're viewing it on your phone, in your hand, and on the plane!

In 1996, when Expedia first started, it was hard to imagine the site as it is today. Travel agents would never have guessed that their industry would be so technologically changed forever. (Please note, this is not saying anything against travel agents.)

Just like every other consumer market, there are some consumers who are not concerned with getting the best bang for the buck, for travel. There are those who never want to plan a trip on their own: they want and need someone to take care of the planning for them. Until the last ten years, most trips required using a booking or travel agent. Of course, before the development of Expedia, you *had* to use a travel agent.

Travelers will continue to use travel agents. This is good for us, the readers of this book. In order to be able to take advantage of hot travel deals out there, we need folks to continue to use travel agents - those who want someone else to do it for them and who do not mind paying full price. It is because of them that we can enjoy huge savings from our plans.

Sometimes fear plays a part in why consumers use travel agents. It can feel scary to them to choose a destination on their own and they worry it will not live up to their standards or travel hopes. It leads them to use a travel agent so they can feel more confident in planning a trip, and they'll have someone to blame if their expectations are not met. The main reason people use travel agents, however, are for ease: they are time savers. We are a busy, technology-infused, rat pack world.

It took the hero of Jules Verne's 1873 novel **'Around the World in Eighty Days'** exactly 80 days to travel around the globe. Why do you think he embarked on such a journey? Adventure? Curiosity? The thrill?

Now we can travel the planet in much less than 80 days, as Jules Verne predicted back in 1873. In the year 2000 we could travel around the world on the Concorde in 22 hours. Less than 24 hours later and boom – we conquered what Jules Verne fantasized about. Of course they retired the Concorde in 2003, but we can end up anywhere on this planet in only twenty-four hours.

If Jules Verne knew how travel has evolved today, I believe his expectations would be that every man, woman, and child would experience the gift of travel as often as they can. Verne would probably have a ticket on an upcoming moon flight.

Traveling is not just for the wealthy, but for those who are dedicated to journeys, seeing the world, and expanding their minds. With the right tools and desire, travel can be done in a smart, economical way. Use this book to find a better, smarter, savvier way to vacation.

So, "Why Travel?" *Why not?* It is easier to plan a trip today than ever before in history. It is exhilarating to find the best bang for your buck, and rewarding when you know that you succeeded in making a great deal and will experience a memory to cherish for the rest of your life.

Opportunities are endless and possibilities are abundant. Technology has opened a new time travel window.

Questions to help you understand "Why Travel?"

1. The last time you took a vacation, how did you feel the first day when you knew work was behind you and you were on your way to your destination?

2. Name one new experience or landmark that you witnessed during your last vacation.

3. When you think back to your favorite vacation memories, what is the first thing that pops into your mind? Write it down.

4. Is it a specific city? A scenic place that was awe-inspiring? Was it a family outing? Did you try out a new sport? What type of vacation was it?

5. What made your favorite vacation memory stand out?

6. How did you feel the day you came back from vacation?

7. How did you feel the next time you decided to book a vacation?

8. How difficult do you think it would be to plan your new favorite vacation?

"Life is either a daring adventure or nothing." -- Helen Keller

Chapter 3

Where to? *So Many Possibilities ...*

So, now you know **why** you want to travel, and you really, really want to travel. In fact, you can't wait. Just thinking about taking a trip is resulting in an overwhelming, stomach-flipping excitement. You are ready to start planning your next vacation by looking up websites and googling your location. You are hit with a burst of adrenaline. Your heart beats a little faster.

All the possibilities start ticking in your mind: flashes of beaches, white sugar sands, ancient stone castles, towering mountains, and luxurious, unique surroundings. Images run through your mind like a motion picture slide show, with an exotic music soundtrack playing in the background and the taste of delectable food in your mouth. The slide show in your mind is like a blur of images on a video presentation at the office that won't stop or pause long enough to read. It plays over and over again.

Wow, which way do I go?

North, South, East, West - endless choices exist. So, like most folks, choosing your next vacation destination requires some thought.

In an experiment, I asked twenty-five friends and colleagues how they picked their last vacation destination. This is what I discovered:

> Ten people replied that price was the main reason for choosing their destination.

> Six stated, "Because I always dreamed of going there."

> Three chose their destination because they were invited to a destination wedding.

> Four replied that the destination was nearby their home, and a good price for a nice resort.

> Two stated that they had been there before and loved it, and did not want to be disappointed by trying somewhere new.

So, what is the right way to choose your vacation? Well, obviously there is not one right or wrong answer. The reason I was able to journey on my 99 vacations in 3 years, however, is because I was open to the **Secret of Possibilities.**

The Secret of Possibilities

The possibilities that exist for traveling are endless! A beautiful old farmhouse in Tuscany. A soft white beach in the Caribbean. Gorgeous majestic mountains and colorful trees to light up your color wheel.

My husband and I have a favorite pastime - well, I suppose we have several; but the one that pertains to this book is talking about travel. Yes, it is exciting to discuss ideas of where to explore. Think of all the thrilling wonders of the world, both manmade and natural. It's kind of hard to focus and stop your mind from wandering when you think of all the possibilities that are out there.

Think to yourself, *where do I want to travel next to experience something new? Where would I like to be right now?*

Sometimes we'd end up talking about a place because we just learned about it in a travel magazine or in catchy conversations from acquaintances - places that sounded unique, exotic, and fun. From personal pampering trips to unbelievable wonders of the world, we would discuss an infinite number of possibilities. Soft white sugary beaches, worn, curving cobblestone pedestrian streets in gothic cities, or a butterfly conservatory located in the middle of a primitive rainforest in Belize - the opportunities are endless.

Perhaps the ideal place is a spot to revisit history or witness a natural wonder that is unbelievable to the human eye and logic unless it's experienced. The vacation could even be a combination of trips: a place to explore and become absorbed in the elements, or one that needs volunteers for a day. A vacation becomes more than you can imagine when you give up just one of your vacation days to help someone from a completely different culture who is less fortunate.

An old favorite saying that has always stuck with me goes something like this: There are those who spend their time talking about others, those who spend their time talking about things, and those who spend their time talking about ideas. Eleanor Roosevelt is cited as making the statement: **"Great minds discuss ideas, average minds discuss events, small minds discuss people."**

This is a good quote to remember. It is a good reminder to always strive to fall in the "great mind" categories and typically not in the category where the only conversation you have is about other people (in other words, gossip).

It is much more exciting to talk about ideas of traveling.

Trying to decide where to go next is exciting. We would share articles or travel channel episodes about our next trips. We would make a list of countries we either have not visited together or have never set foot on. We purchased a large map of the world and marked the places we visited and places we would like to go, using different colored push pins. Red was the place we wanted to visit and cool blue meant we have already touched down in that part of the world. We would write down the top five places we would like to visit next.

The answers were not all dream scenarios. They were in three categories: big trip, medium trip or little trips. Depending on the criteria, there would be different answers.

What defines a Big Trip? To our minds, a big trip was one that took longer to accomplish from our home base. Our home base today is Arizona. Because the travel time is longer on big trips, they tend to be more expensive trips, due in part to the fact that we may want to stay a little longer. Since the travel time was more extensive and cost more, we categorized this as a "big trip". A big trip was not a weekend getaway.

Medium trips could be a weekend getaway or even a less expensive trip without extensive travel time.

A little trip is any time you get away, go away, and discover somewhere new. Little trips can occur all year round without a lot of cost and time.

Generally, if you're like most of us, a few elementary questions pop up in your head. What does your calendar look like for the upcoming year? When would be a good time to travel and take vacation time off from work? How is the weather in that part of the world at that time? Is it high season or low season for that country?

Being organized and looking at the above questions from the beginning will help you think about where to go and give you a general idea of when to go. This will help you narrow down the possibilities. Okay, let's think about where you want to go on your upcoming vacations. Take the time to answer the questions below. I promise that this will help you visualize some ideas. Planning and organizing are key elements to taking more vacations.

One idea that really helps you gather your possible vacations together is to have a notebook, journal, or logbook to help you think about your travels. Our travel journal has several different parts. We have a list in the front of the book with all the trips we have taken and their dates. We have a Section Two listing all the places we want to travel to, and we cross it out as we visit each destination.

If you are a list person, you will get some sweet satisfaction out of the crossing or checking off the list part. Vacations are an important part of life, so what are you waiting for? Go grab the notebook at the dollar store and start a travel journal that you will have with you for a lifetime.

Questions to help you decide where your next vacation will be:

1. How did you choose your last vacation destination?

2. In your top ten travel bucket list, which trip seems the easiest?

3. Which travel bucket list seems the most impossible?

4. List the things you want to do on a vacation.

5. How will you pay for it?

Okay, let's look at the first question, "How did you choose your last vacation destination?" Was it an invitation from friends or family? Was it a place that you always wanted to go to? Did you see a good deal advertised and then decided that at that price, you could afford to go?

Now, go to your travel log or the list you made of your travel bucket list from Chapter 1 and ask yourself which trip on your list seems the easiest to accomplish?

Which trip on your travel bucket list seems the hardest? Why? Is it cost? Is it travel time? Think about what makes this trip difficult. Taking a closer look at any problems or issues will help break them down so you can resolve them. Think of ways you can resolve some of the issues. Write this down: remember, we are brainstorming possibilities.

Now look at the things you enjoy doing on vacation, or that you love to do when you have the time off. What do they have in common? Where can you do these things? Do they match any of your bucket list places? If not, think about where you can do your favorite things on vacation near where you live. This would be a small trip. Think about where you can do your favorite activities in exotic places. Most likely, these will be your big trips.

Look at your list of possibilities and try to figure out a ballpark estimate of costs. How will you pay for it? If the answer comes easy, great! If not, read Chapters 5, 9 and 10 on ways to go green and save enough money for a vacation, and how to take inexpensive trips, all for a tank of gas.

The secret of possibilities is endless. Start talking more about vacations and ideas when you're out having dinner with friends. Find out where others have traveled. Have a favorite movie or book with stunning scenery and magical places where you can picture yourself in that scene. Find out where it is located.

The secret of possibilities is that you have the ability to go anywhere in the world with a little planning and inspiration.

"Two roads diverged in a wood and I – I took the one less traveled by." – **Robert Frost**

Chapter 4: When is the best time to travel?

The correct answer would be that anytime is a good time for vacation. Planning ahead with some flexibility, however, can assist in saving $$ and adding enjoyment to the journey.

There are many times of the year the travel industry would categorize as "the best time to travel." Usually these involve looking for off-peak times (or "shoulder times," as they are sometimes called by travel agents). Last minute trip planning, when done at the right time of year, can offer amazing savings. Basically, if you are flexible, there are numerous hot deals to be had at the last minute.

Let's start with the beginning of the year.

Most folks don't realize it, but January is on the top of the list for "best month for travel deals."

Resort towns and travel industry experts know that January comes with New Year's resolutions. It is a good time for everyone to start out with a clean slate and make some goals for the New Year. Whether it is designing a new household budget, losing weight, or completing new adventures, this is an opportune time to sit down and write out your goals for the year - work goals, family goals, and personal goals.

Travel industry experts know this, so to jump start their new year, they offer wonderful incentives, packages, and free nights, after the holidays. As a result, January 5th and on will showcase some tempting incentives; especially if you book a trip at the end of the previous year (in December) or caught a deal on the famous Black Friday and Cyber Monday the year before. Yes, even the travel industry is getting into Black Friday deals. If you plan and have a travel strategy, you will catch some of the lowest prices and jump start your new goals for the year.

Perhaps before you get a piece of paper out and start writing down your New Year's resolutions, you should make a resolution to add travel to the list, right now. It will start the year off right and put you and your significant others at the top of the priority list instead of (as unfortunately happens) seeing 'travel' fall to last on the list.

Are you a list person? I make a list every morning, and if you pulled my crumpled lists out of the garbage, you would see travel on my to-do list, every week. Planning it is almost as much fun as doing it (almost); so make a new spot on your to-do list, to include travel planning. If you plan it, it will come. This is a true statement. How many times do we talk about going somewhere, see the great deal, and then wish later that we had just planned it? If you plan it, I guarantee that your year will have some added pleasures.

Here are some tips to knowing when the best time to travel is:

1. Check out the high peak and off-peak times of the destination you are traveling to. **If you see when the break is between the two times, it is always good to book right before the high peak and at the end of the low point.** This way, you are almost visiting your destination at the super expensive time; but by booking a few days before or after the high peak starts or ends, you will have saved money by not paying the highest rate. It allows you to enjoy the same accommodations at a much lower price than the travelers who will be staying there the next week, or who have stayed the week before. The extra savings can afford you *two* trips this year, instead of one.

2. Check out the time frame of the off-peak seasons at a few of the destinations you're thinking about visiting. **Why is it off-peak?** Is it because it is a skiing destination and the ski season is not in swing? Is it during school sessions, and not at a convenient time when the kids are on vacation? Perhaps it has to do with weather, schedules, and events. Stop a minute and think about this. What if you decide to look outside the box? Go on a trip to a beautiful ski

town in the summer. It may be a great opportunity to stay in fabulous resorts or hotels at low, low rates and explore the town without the crowds. Most ski towns are breathtakingly beautiful year round. Make it a hiking and spa vacation instead of a skiing vacation and you will get to explore the town, eat at the same great eateries, and sleep in the same luxury beds at half the price. Plus, checking it out pre-season will let you know if you want to come back to the destination for skiing at the higher prices.

3. The same tips apply to summertime peak season locations. **If you are traveling without children, check out the time of year when most children are in school.** You may find special deals and discounts. Most locations that cater to families and children during the summer months have great rates off-season. Sometimes a midyear vacation can turn out to be a highly educational adventure for your children. If you are an empty nester or without children, look at these times for hot rates.

4. **Travel during the week, not weekends, if your schedule allows this.** Typically leaving or departing mid-week can save you money on both transportation and accommodations. You may even discover that coming back on a Friday or a Saturday allows you to have a day of rest before the new week starts.

5. **Do a little gambling when you book your next vacation.** Check out resorts that have gambling and

see when their low occupancy rates are. I guarantee that if you go to their websites and sign up for special promotions throughout the year, you will be emailed their latest promotions. Sign up for their player's card, and read the emails. Even if you are not a gambler, there are great resorts, award-winning restaurants, and shopping, in gambling areas. Typically, casino resorts have luxury appeal and great excursions that have nothing to do with gambling. Laughlin, Nevada is a perfect example. Laughlin is a mini Las Vegas along the Colorado River in Nevada offering four-star hotels at $20 - $30 a night during the week or off season. Even if you're not a gambler, they have golf courses, swimming pools along the Colorado, river cruises, and an old west town (Oatman, AZ, on Route 66) within 20 miles of the casino; not to mention the fact that most casinos offer gourmet restaurants, movie theaters, and outlet shopping nearby. Las Vegas also offers great room prices and is the gateway to The Grand Canyon, Sedona, AZ, and California vacations. If you are interested in entertainment, stay for the shows, not the gambling. *Hot tip*: If you do like to gamble, make sure you get a casino card. The Cosmopolitan in Las Vegas is a 5-star casino with rooms at $300 a night (can't beat the fountain rooms facing the Bellagio water show). They give you points for restaurant dollars, the spa, and room rates, and after one stay, they send you specials with a variety of discounts, free nights, and dining credits.

6. **Take a last-minute chance**. This trick may be hard for those who need to feel secure and organized ahead of time. Be an adventurer; try this method for one trip. Basically, patience is the name of the game. You have to wait until the last minute to book your room, but trust me: it usually pays off. If it is a driving destination you are visiting, then airfare prices will not be an issue. If it is a destination for which you need to purchase an airline ticket, use hipmunk.com, Kayak.com, or bookingbuddy.com and complete an "alert" for the month you want to fly. Bing.com will tell you what the best time is currently for the lowest fare available (more detail on this in Chapter 7). If you put in an alert through your email address, they will search for lower fares from your city of departure to your destination and then will email you when a fare drops. It works great, but when you see a lower fare, be ready to purchase your ticket. It is okay to buy airfare early if you've researched the prices by using the websites, and know that it is a good deal. The gamble is that you haven't booked your room, yet. Take a breath; it will be all right. Don't book your room right away. Wait until a few weeks before you go. You will be amazed at the deals that will surface at the last minute. It may be a little worrisome, for some, not having firm plans; but try it out. You do have the option of tentatively booking a place online that has a 72-hour or less cancellation policy. Expedia, Booking, Travelocity, and some other travel websites guarantee a 100% refund within a certain time frame. Having a booked backup may help you feel

more comfortable instead of waiting until the last minute. This is especially true if you are not flexible with your schedule and must pick a specific time in high season. Typically, high season travel requires a different approach. Remember: if you book a room with free cancellation while you search for lower fares, note it on your calendar with an alert, so you remember to cancel it.

7. **High season/special event booking.** If you are making a reservation for a specific event – and generally, special events fall in high season – then booking earlier is better. Once again: you can check out the cancellation policy and if you find a better option at the last minute, then notify the hotel to see if they will match the rate. Sometimes you just need to ask, or book the better rate and then cancel. Planning is recommended and important when your travel is not flexible, when you're attending a special occasion, or during high season.

Try this: Grab a monthly calendar (or print out a monthly calendar online). Go to freecalendars.com and you can print out a twelve-month block calendar. Pick a weekend out of every month for the next year that you will plan to take a vacation.

Remember: travel doesn't have to mean taking big, expensive vacations. Read the last chapter on ten trips you can take for just a tank of gas, and plan a few of those during the year. Planning really helps you decide when to take a vacation, and organization insures that you will take a vacation. Go through the monthly calendar and write the word "Trip" on one weekend a month. Go back through the yearly calendar and write "Big" beside Trip on at least one, two, or three of the weekends – whatever your goal is for the year.

Now, be flexible on where you want to go, and check out the off-peak season times or shoulder times of your favorite destinations. After you do this exercise, you will have a sketched-out yearly plan for vacations. Planning can be almost as much fun as the vacation and can help reduce stress from your life by organizing healthy adventures and relaxation.

If you use iCalender or Outlook, take five minutes and go through each month and schedule thirty minutes in your calendar each week to go over vacation plans. Remember: you are worth it, and so are your friends and family. If you can spend thirty minutes at the water cooler or watching an episode of a Netflix series, you can spend thirty minutes a week to plan a vacation. This is a valuable secret: try it out for one month and see what happens.

So, if you're looking for an after-holiday stress release and a way to get away after the big celebrations, then check out the above strategies and start the new decade off with travel (isn't that one of your New Year's resolutions?) If not, make sure you add that to the list this year. It is sure to improve your year and your life!)

"One's destination is never a place, but a new way of seeing things." -- Henry Miller

Chapter 5: *How do I afford it?*

Money, is the one travel necessity we must take with us (at least a little bit). Whether it is Hamilton, Jackson, Grant or Franklin going on the trip with you, here's the inside information to making those old men work for less

Okay, now for the big question on most of your minds: $$$$$. MONEY!

You understand *why* to travel. You understand even *where* to travel (even though there are so **many** places to choose from). Using time management ideas from the last chapter, you can even figure out *when* to travel. Your mind is exploding with ideas of places you want to see in this lifetime. Underneath it all, however, is the big question, HOW DO I AFFORD IT?

Three words... Research, Save, and Plan.

Research

This book will give you research tools to secure the best price on your vacations. Chapter 7 will lead you to websites that will assist in conducting your research quickly and efficiently.

Yes, research takes time. If money is not an issue for you, however, and you don't have the time, then you may just want to call a travel agent and have them help you. Travel agents can tell you, in one call, what price is available for your dream destination, and you can book it! If this sounds great to you and your capital is plentiful, then by all means, go ahead. This is certainly a good option for folks with a plethora of cash. It is also a time-saving option - but not a cheaper option. A travel secret worth knowing: to save cash, plan vacations on your own. Besides the moolah you save, the benefits and sense of satisfaction are endless.

Researching a destination is part of the adventure. Perhaps I think of myself as a perpetual student. If research brings up bad school day memories, stop for a second and realize that this is fun research - research which will get you excited about your upcoming dream destination.

Once you try it, you will realize there is something distinctive about researching a destination on your own, locating that one special place to stay or visit, a not-so-touristy spot, or a place even tour groups are not going to visit - something a little off the beaten path or unmistakably unique, new, or unusual. Or it can involve finding the new hip hot spot that is within walking distance to everything, near a really happening scene.

Researching the destination and familiarizing yourself with maps and locations of hot spots to see really expands your geographical knowledge base and teaches you more about your destination. One of my favorite quotes by Ralph Waldo Emerson, "Life is a journey, not a destination," speaks clearly to me on several levels.

Basically, enjoy the journey while you are on your way to the destination. This means: enjoy **all** the parts: planning, researching, and saving for your next trip. Researching and educating yourself on the destination will save you money and enhance the time it takes to get there. So yes, the journey is much more than going from Point A to Point B. The journey is the *entire process* of the vacation, from researching to traveling, enjoying the destination, and making the trip home.

Saving money

Saving for your vacation is also part of the journey, and planning it out on your own can be an important piece that helps save you money.

What you may experience while researching your destination, saving, and planning for your trip is an added benefit that only costs you thirty minutes a week.

Get a piggy bank or an empty jar and tape the name of your destination on it. Make a point to drop in lose change, a dollar bill, or even a few fives, from time to time. As you watch the bank fill up, you'll realize you have something fun and rewarding to look forward to. If you spend time researching the destination and you personally plan the adventure, when you get there, you will feel a little more confident in the place and your decision. It is like gaining a free perk of self-confidence and learning. Having a vested interest in your destination and how you are paying for it is a trip in itself. If you've never tried this approach, what do you have to lose?

In tough economic times, everyone becomes creative in trying to stretch the dollar. Everyone becomes inventive on ways to save money. From the Coupon Mom blogger to the financial advice segments on the *Today Show*, everyone is giving advice and suggestions, if you listen. Most of us have learned new tricks on how to save money over the past few years. Just when we think we have heard it all, we find a new way to save; even when we thought it wasn't possible.

A certain amount of peace and satisfaction comes with saving money, but satisfaction is threefold when you are saving money for a vacation!!!

Here are some ideas on how to save money for your trip:

1. **Buy a piggy bank, a large bottle, a jar, a vase, or use an empty water bottle and start collecting loose change**. Make it a rule to never carry loose change (men – in your pockets; or women – in the bottom of your purse). Make a new habit where, every night, you empty out all pockets and

purses and put the change in the big vase or water bottle or piggy bank. In a year, you may be amazed at what you've saved.

2. **Help the earth, save some money.** Read the suggestions on going green in Chapter 10, and implement a few of them in your life. By helping the environment and yourself, you will save money for a trip that normally wouldn't receive a second thought.

3. **Set up a secret savings account with your bank** or **credit union**. This is a savings account you won't monitor or look at. Just forget about it. If your employer has a direct deposit option, you can elect to take a small amount out of each paycheck and have it deposited to your secret savings account. Ask them not to send you a monthly statement. Usually they can send you one quarterly or twice a year, depending on your banking institution. In six months, you may be amazed at how much you saved for your vacation. Make sure you check all the bank rules for fees, so you are not adding any unnecessary expenses to your savings.

4. **Start a vacation club savings account.** Remember the days when banks offered Christmas Club savings accounts? (Yes, they really did!) The idea behind it was to deposit what you could afford over the course of the year and then use it for Christmas presents. Well, start a Vacation Club savings account... call it whatever you like. This one doesn't have to be secret, but when you are

depositing a check or have extra money, just place it in the vacation savings account. The idea is to put it away and don't touch it, except for vacations.

5. **Stop the Starbucks - or at least, cut back**... I know that may be extremely hard for some; but just try cutting back. I'm not against Starbucks. If you are one of those folks, however, who purchase several coffees a week, try to cut down to one a week and make your own coffee. Think about the trade-off... more vacations, less Starbucks. Do the math: if you are drinking three or four a week, you could save $500 to $600 for a vacation just by adjusting to less Starbucks. Perhaps it's not a Starbucks coffee that gets you reaching into your pocket every week, but a fountain drink with lunch every day or midday in the afternoon; or a beer at a bar instead of at home. Whatever your constant habit is, try to do a little less of it to save some money for vacation. If it cost you $10- $12 a week, try skipping it, replacing it with something from home or something less expensive, and start saving. Once again: you can save $500-$600 a year for vacation.

6. If you use credit cards, **check out your travel awards**. This is worth investigating. Many banks, hotels, and resort chains offer credit cards with points with no blackout dates and at least $1 per 1-point redemption. If you are an organized and disciplined person, you can easily do this, and it can pay off. Buy monthly expenses on the same credit card and pay it off every month. Think of it as a debit card. Set a monthly allowance or budget for those

essential items, use the card, then pay it off every month. In a year, you should have enough for at least one airfare ticket.

7. Use the websites or travel apps in Chapter 7 to check your prices on trips, before you purchase... it does pay off. Never book a trip without checking at least two other websites: go to Trivago, Trip Advisor, and Expedia. Do this in your thirty-minute weekly allocated travel time.

8. Read Chapter 6, "**99 Secrets That Will Change The Way You Travel And Save You Money,**" **then use at least 25% of them in some way this year. You will save money.**

9. Read Chapter 10 and plan a few vacations that you can take for a tank of a gas. Taking a few smaller vacations each year allows you to save money for a few larger, more expensive vacations. It is still a vacation no matter how close in distance it is, and will help you explore and try new things.

10. Check for seasonal jobs during the holiday season. If you're up for putting in some extra work for a short period, try getting a seasonal or part-time work-from-home job. You may meet new people or learn about a new destination. Regardless, you will earn extra money. In just a month or two you can earn enough for a vacation. Work hard to play hard.

11. Have you ever thought about eBay? It works for an astonishing number of folks. Begin by organizing a

few boxes of stuff you have in storage, in the attic, or in the basement. Try their online program, to sell your used items to people who want them, and try to sell items that you have no use for. It may help you simplify your home and life as you start saving for a vacation. There are apps that also do this, as well as Craigslist.

12. Check out the section in Chapter 7, on Airbnb. You can make money by being a host to guests in your residence. If this is a possibility for your residence, sign up to be a host, and offer to rent a room. This might be your new ticket to earning money for your vacation.

Plan

Remember the "if you plan it, it will come" saying? You can do all the research in the world about a place and learn a wealth of interesting facts and locations. You can save for years for that special vacation and have multiple travel savings accounts to be proud of, and an overflowing piggy bank. If you do not plan the vacation, however, it may never happen.

After you have finished researching your next exciting destination, write it down and get ready to follow through with a plan. You are now probably having colorful dreams at night, about exciting destinations.

Finally: your piggy bank is full and your money is saved - pick a DATE to go! Give notice at work, take your vacation days, and make it official. Now you can decide if you want to plan everything on your trip, wait to the last moment, or play it by ear.

Picking a date is important, and by scheduling vacation time at work, you will be committed. Now, do one more thing to make each trip exciting. Try it just once. Do a countdown on your bathroom mirror: buy one pad of sticky notes (bright yellow or any bright colors are great to use from the dollar store). Number each sticky note with a number of your choice (you can break apart the sticky notes or use the whole pad, starting with 1 at the bottom of the pad, and rip one off each day) ... 90 days to go ... 89 days to go...When you get down to ten days, you will be enthusiastic, ready and organized.

Where will your next trip be? Plan it, pick the date, buy the sticky notes, and get excited!

The unexpected can happen, and that is good. Having a well-organized plan and ideas of where to vacation is the key to going from just thinking about a destination to actually visiting the exotic locale in person. A travel notebook, travel logs, or journals can really assist you in planning. A travel calendar is a "must".

Think about the important events and appointments in your life. You plan for and write them on your calendar with scheduled times to make sure you show up. Well, vacations will not happen by themselves. Make time every week for your vacation planning - this will save you money. Treat this as just important as that teeth cleaning every six months. Plan it, and it will come.

"For my part, I travel not to go anywhere, but to go. I travel for travel's sake. The great affair is to move." – Robert Louis Stevenson

Chapter 6

99 Secrets That Will Change The Way You Travel And Save You Money

Below are 99 secrets that will save you money on your next vacation. Read through the list and highlight the ones you are not doing, then try out a few on your next trip. These secrets will enhance your journey and take less out of your pocket so you can travel more.

1. Before you book a vacation directly from the hotel or travel agent, check your travel package on Expedia and Trip Advisor, making sure you've booked the lowest rate.

2. Be flexible with the days you travel. Do you really need to leave on Friday and return on Sunday for every weekend trip?

3. Book mid-week stays in touristy areas.
4. Book weekend stays in business areas.
5. Buy city metro or day passes ahead of time.
6. See if large cities offer a City Pass to popular tourist destinations.
7. Google Groupon and the city you are traveling to and discover which restaurants, shows, or tourist attractions have deep discounts.
8. Travel with a cooler.
9. Buy bottled water at a grocery store or pharmacy instead of buying overpriced water bottles from a mini-bar.
10. Travel with small bottles of liquor.
11. Stop at the local grocery store and buy supplies.
12. Take along breakfast bars or easy travel snacks such as nuts, bars, or string cheese.
13. Plan to eat several meals on your own, during the trip - a breakfast bar, for a few mornings; or eat two meals out a day instead of three. Splurge on the other two!
14. Seek local restaurants off the beaten path instead of automatically choosing touristy dining destinations that are pricey.
15. See if the resort or hotel offers food and beverage delivery, before you arrive. Some of the best

moments of a trip are arriving to cold beverages in your refrigerator, and you enjoy a cocktail on your deck or patio.

16. Buy show tickets online before you go. Most theatre productions have discount tickets when you buy ahead of time.

17. Pick up the local newspaper or tourist guide and look for coupons.

18. Sign up for a hotel rewards card before you go, to earn points. You may receive preferred check-in, a free newspaper, or members-only perks, upon check-in.

19. Tell the hotel, if it is a special celebration, when you book. Hotels are very receptive to anniversaries, birthdays, and special celebrations. Often they may offer preferred rooms, free upgrades, and sometimes a special treat like a free bottle of champagne or chocolate-covered strawberries.

20. Call the hotel directly when you have decided where you are staying *before* you hit the Expedia button to buy the reservation. It pays to place the call and double-check that the hotel can't beat the online price. You will only know this by asking directly.

21. Use public transportation: it's very inexpensive, and a unique way to see the inner workings of a city.

22. Check to see if the town or village you're visiting has horse and buggy rides or a unique form of

transportation. Typically, the driver can cite historical legends or spin local tales you may not hear on the bus. This is a great place to start your overview of the city.

23. Forgo the rental car and walk. If you are traveling to a walkable city, don't rent a car. Stroll, strut, and trek your way through it like a local.

24. Check ahead with the hotel to understand their overnight parking charges. A big mistake travelers make is not checking parking rates. A great hotel deal that has a $25 per diem charge for parking may no longer be a great travel deal.

25. If the hotel does charge high overnight parking fees, check online for areas around the hotel that offer free or cheaper parking. Websites like Trip Advisor usually will have traveler suggestions on cheap parking.

26. Bid on Hotwire for rental cars. Check your rental car site of choice, figure out the cheapest price, and then bid lower using Hotwire.

27. Reserve the cheapest car category you can tolerate. At the car rental place, ask if there are any specials, any deals on upgrades, or any other alternatives available. Check Expedia a few days before your trip to see if the car you booked has decreased. You can generally cancel rental cars at any time, except on Priceline, where cars are prepaid and non-cancellable. Book the lower price and cancel the higher one.

28. Like to write? Write travel stories and earn some free perks for traveling. Look up www.thewriterslife.com and http://www.writersincharge.com for ideas/advice on how to make money writing.

29. Don't be the traveler who buys souvenirs for everyone on the trip. Your friends and family didn't go on the trip, and most of the time that little souvenir you bought for them (i.e. the miniature Eiffel tower key chain) will soon be forgotten.

30. If you must give travel souvenirs, send postcards. With snail mail becoming an archaic form of communication, a handwritten postcard will mean volumes. Lazy? There's even an app that will do it for you. Check out the Postino app. You can snap the photo, sign your name, and write your message on your phone. A postcard will arrive to its destination in less than a week!

31. Another great idea for those who want to give a travel souvenir to friends and family: Before departing on your vacation, go to the dollar store and buy 5x7 frames that hold 4x6 pictures. Make a sign before you leave: "Hi, Mom, I'm in Paris (or London, or the Bahamas), and I'm thinking of you!" Take a great photo of you holding the sign, or a great scenic shot with the sign in the picture... print it out when you get home, make copies, and give them to your friends and family. It's a priceless gift that will put a smile on their faces and save you time and money. As

a bonus, you will have less to carry around on your journey and to smash in your suitcase on the way home.

32. Invest in a good backpack, purse, or murse (man's purse) to carry around and hold travel treasures, camera, snacks, and a bottle of water. When your blood sugar is low and you need something quick to eat, you will have it accessible without being stuck somewhere or having to pay $5 for a bottle of water.

33. Pick your credit card of choice and sign up for their rewards program, and use it consistently. Charge all your monthly expenses on this card. If you are disciplined enough to pay it off every month and reap the points, then in a year you should have enough for a free airline ticket, hotel room, etc.

34. Take advantage of airline frequent flyer programs. You can sign up for free. Spend a half hour one day and sign up for every airline. Keep the numbers in your phone under "notes". Never fly without entering a frequent flyer number or renting a car and using an airline partner. Someday they will add up, and with airline mergers, others become unexpected alliance partners.

35. Bid on travel auctions. Check out travel auction sites such as Skyauction.com and Priceline, but always read the fine print.

36. Take a bag lunch with you to the airport. Shop at your favorite deli or make a great homemade sandwich and pack it up with some nuts, treats, and

protein bars. It will be a third of the cost of the airport's food prices, and probably healthier. A little portable cooler will be handy on the trip.

37. Go to the library prior to departure and check out travel books instead of buying a new travel book for $25-$30. The library generally has travel guides from several publishers: if you find one you really love, then buy it used online or at a used book store.

38. Check out the CD lending section at your library. Find the country you are visiting and check out some local music. You can download music and listen to it before you go, to get in the mood.

39. Make a travel playlist of free local music from the library and listen to songs on the journey while on the plane, train, or car. This will get you in the moment of the wonderful journey you are about to embark on. In the future, when you hear the music, it will transport you back to those good feelings of your journey.

40. Google the movies made on location in the area you are traveling to. Watch a few before you leave for the trip and they will provide some great insights into your destination and will get you excited for the trip. (It was an amazing experience to watch the film of Anne Frank, for example, before visiting the real location in Amsterdam).

41. Check out free DVDs from the lending area of your public library. Take a few with you and on late

nights during your travels, fall asleep to a great film. You are on vacation - relax.

42. Make sure you have chargers, batteries, and extra memory cards with you before you leave. Buying camera accessories while traveling can get very expensive.

43. Invest in an inexpensive travel tripod. For $20-$30, you can buy a very compact tripod that is bendable, and if you're traveling in groups, pairs, or even as an individual, you can have photos with all of you in them. Go to Amazon.com. They have flexible travel tripods for under $20. There's also a selfie stick for under $15 which works great if you are traveling alone or as a couple.

44. Clean out and delete bad pictures on your camera before you arrive home. Whether flying in a plane, train, or car, spend the time on the return trip to go through your digital pictures and delete those that are shaky, duplicates, too dark, not in focus, etc. If you do this at the end of each day, it will help you prevent the scenario of returning home only to realize you have taken 900 photos on vacation - and when will you have the time to go through them?

45. When you have internet access or public wi-fi at the hotel, upload your pictures to the cloud, just in case something happens to your phone or camera.

46. On photo websites, you can choose the option to make a photo book. Most have an app for your phone (Walmart, Costco, Walgreens). This is a great way to

have 100 pictures in a keepsake book that you can show to family and friends when you get home.

47. Download your photos to your smart TV, dvd player, or computer. This is another great way to show photos to friends and family. Have family members over, and play it in the background.

48. Google your destination for any special events happening at the time you are traveling. It can be frustrating to travel to a location, only to realize your favorite band is playing, but the tickets are sold out. If you had done the research ahead of time, you would have been prepared. Ask the hotel where you are staying if they have any tickets.

49. Check out free events at your destination. Large cities, small towns, and villages generally have websites showcasing events open to the community.

50. Check out special art exhibits, community events, and historical landmarks open to the public.

51. Make an old-fashioned picnic to enjoy while on vacation. If you are bringing a backpack, go to a local market and buy some local bread, cheese, and fruit - perhaps a bottle of wine. Small, light airline blankets are good to keep in the backpack when traveling. Find a place to take a walk or a hike or even a local park, and have lunch or dinner. Who knows: this may end up being one of your favorite vacation moments. Don't forget to snap a photo.

52. Are you a wine drinker? Take advantage of the local wineries. Before leaving for your trip, Google local wineries. Given the popularity of wineries, you never know where a new winery has started. Many wineries offer free wine tasting, tours of the vineyard, and interesting facts about the area.

53. Understand the local flavor of the town you are visiting. If the town used to be an old gold mining town, research old mines that are open to the public. If the town is known for a certain product, see where they make it. Many factories have free tours open to the public. In Mismaloya, Mexico, near Puerto Vallarta, the small town lets you tour a tequila factory, taste the tequila, and swing an axe at an agave plant.

54. Ask about walking tours. Generally, there is a free city guide that will list folks who make their living conducting walking tours. Fodor's, Lonely Planet, and other travel publications offer a section with suggested walking tours you can do on your own. Once again: before you leave, use the internet and Google walking tours for your specific destination. (Download HearPlanet, as mentioned in Chapter 7).

55. Budget food money for the day. Plan, each day, how many meals you are going to eat at a restaurant. Are you going to eat out for all three meals; or one very special meal? Use protein bars for breakfast and some bread, cheese, and fruit for lunch.

56. Understand the local produce and products of the town. Wander through a local market, not a tourist

convenience store, and see what they have that is fresh and unique. The local market will be very inexpensive and is often a wonderful travel memory.

57. Don't be intimidated about trying the local shops, even if you do not speak the language. The language of buy and sell needs no words. If you find something you want and have the money to buy it, the transaction will happen.

58. Buy some packaged local sauces; seasonings you can take back home. Olive oils at the local market or some soup seasonings can really help you relive your trip when you get home. These also makes great, inexpensive mementos. Buy a seasoning, and when you're home, print out a local recipe that uses that seasoning—these make great gifts.

59. Videoshoot important trip details you want to remember but not write down. In Belize, I was given an incredible recipe; so I hit "video" and recorded the instructions. When I came home, I could recreate the recipe with the spices I'd purchased in Belize.

60. If staying at a resort-style location, ask if they offer activities. Check out the calendar and plan ahead. One free event offered at a resort in Puerto Vallarta was the hatching of baby turtles and releasing them into the ocean. Offered at the kids' center, it was open to all guests. Whether you are a kid or at kid at heart, it was a life-changing experience to hold a newborn baby sea turtle and set him free in the sand, cheering him on his way to the sea.

61. Before booking travel excursions through the hotel, do your pre-trip homework and make sure there is not a large surcharge from going direct. Quite often you can have the same trip as other residents of the hotel, but at a discounted rate, if you go direct. Other times the hotel receives a discount for volume. Know before you book.

62. Check out the free sports equipment, recreational equipment, and services offered at your hotel or resort. This can be a great money saver and can allow you to explore your travel location using various modes of transportation. Many beach resorts offer free bicycles, kayaks, small boats, and snorkeling gear. Create your own adventure without paying a tour group for things you can use for free.

63. Many hotels offer free airport pick-up and drop off services which will save you the hassle of a taxi driver's taking advantage of an out-of-town visitor. Contact your hotel ahead of time to save money. Check to see if Uber is in the city you are visiting. This eliminates the possibility of taxi drivers overcharging visitors.

64. Check to see if the hotel offers shuttles into town or other tourist destinations. Hotels and resorts will often shuttle guests to restaurants they recommend or to sister hotels where you can use their amenities. Even if you don't see one listed on the website, ask. Most resorts have some type of shuttle you'll learn about if you inquire.

65. Spend a day volunteering in the local community of the area you are visiting. Most of us don't have free time unless we are on vacation. Before you leave for the trip, ask the resort if they work with any community charities and ask if they can assist you in volunteering for a day. This is one of the best ways to learn and understand your new destination and the people. Who knows, this may lead you to another new adventure or will add to your life through giving back.

66. Get your vacation exercise by walking around the closest shopping area and window shopping, the first day. It will help your jet lag if you have traveled far and will save you a little money, allowing you an opportunity to check out the local wares first rather than buying on impulse.

67. Learn how to barter, if the country is known to do so. In certain parts of the world, bartering is a fun part of the buying process.

68. Buy local. Trinkets, touristy souvenirs you can buy everywhere, and many of other items are offered at home. With a little research, figure out what is handmade locally and find something you like that is original and authentic to the region.

69. Read up on the history of the area you are visiting. Read the history section of the travel book featuring your destination, or just Google the history of the location. You may be surprised what you'll learn

about where you are going. This often inspires local sightseeing to off-the-beaten-track, unique places.

70. Take advantage of hotels and resorts that offer free breakfast. Unless it is your last meal, it will save you money for the meal of the day you will splurge on. Know ahead of time how it works, where it is located, and the times of the free breakfast.

71. Before you leave, Google "special offers and your destination city." You never know...

72. Google the phrase "promotional codes and your hotel name."

73. When researching your destination spot, find out when high or peak season is. Ask the resort, or search it online. Book the week before high season starts or the week after it ends. You will save money and avoid all the crowds.

74. If having a few cocktails on vacation is your type of thing, check out the all-inclusive packages at hotels or resorts. If you are a vacation drinker, book an all-inclusive resort for a few days and get your fill before moving on to a standard accommodation. Calculate what you would spend drinking and eating; the all-inclusive is usually hard to beat, if it's priced right.

75. For those who care more about the destination and love meeting all types of people, check out www.couchsurfing.org. You will not only stay in a local home, but have a few interesting experiences for free. Yes, I said free! You might take the host out to dinner or share a meal, but the use of the couch is

not charged. Another one is hospitalityclub.org. Connect with a network of travelers all over the world.

76. Check out local hiking trails, get some exercise, and see some hidden places. Generally, they are free and good for the heart and mind.

77. Walk, walk, and walk some more. It's free, a great way to exercise, and you never know what interesting sights and people you may stumble upon.

78. Take the road less traveled. Little narrow streets may look like they lead to nowhere, but adventures start on the road less traveled.

79. Use bing.com, hipmunk.com or kayak.com to monitor the cheapest flights to destinations you want to travel to. They have monthly charts listing cheaper times to travel.

80. Use the free travel alerts on bing.com, hipmunk.com, or kayak.com. You can set up free daily or weekly email alerts to let you know when prices have dropped by $25 or more.

81. Order appetizers at local eateries instead of full-course menu items. You will gain the opportunity to taste more exotic and local foods at a cheaper price.

82. Traveling with a group or as a couple? Order an entrée and split it. If you're hungry after the tasting, then try another restaurant and do it again, or go for dessert tasting. After all, you're on vacation.

83. Traveling by plane? When arriving at the airport, go to the ticket counter and ask if you can be put on a list of volunteers in case of oversold flights. They will still get you to your destination, and you will receive a free flight for the future, or airline vouchers. Be flexible with your arrival and departure times so you can take advantage of oversold flights. Do you earn $300-$500 in a few hours? If not, volunteer every time and you are sure to get free future vacation flights. Several airline companies will ask you about this option when you check in. Take advantage of this, get there early, and ask to be added to the list of volunteers.

84. Use VRBO.com and Airbnb (as mentioned in the next chapter). This will save you money not only on food and higher hotel costs, but will allow you to stay in a relaxed environment with all the comforts of home. The owners generally live in the same town and are a great source of information on local secrets. If you have never tried this option, you'll be happy you did.

85. When renting a vehicle, opt out of the added insurance coverage unless you do not have personal car insurance. Generally, personal auto insurance will cover you. Check with your insurance agent.

86. Check with the rental car company about the price of pre-paying to refill your car. Note how many miles you plan to drive versus a tank of gas. If you time it correctly, you can save money on gas.

87. Check with your credit card company to see if they offer rental auto insurance. Typically, this is already a benefit.

88. Take advantage of all the perks the credit card offers for travelers. Call or look it up online. Credit card companies offer some roadside assistance, concierge service, and other travel benefits which most people are unaware of unless you think to ask or research the benefits.

89. If traveling internationally, check if your credit card charges a fee for currency exchange. Find a credit card that will not charge you international fees; then use this card as much as you can during your trip, and you will receive the best exchange rate for the day. A simple phone call or checking the website will answer currency charge questions.

90. Pack a few large padded envelopes (8.5 x11) addressed to your home. While vacationing, you can fill the envelopes with souvenirs that you wish to take back and mail them before you leave, at the slowest rate. It is a nice surprise when it arrives, and saves you room in your luggage.

91. Make a list of the clothes you will wear each day, and stick to the list. This helps with over-packing - and remember, on vacation you want to generally pack for comfort with clothes that you can mix or match easily. Clothes of the same color or basic shades of black, khaki, and white mix easily.

92. Buy super jumbo plastic zip lock bags. You will be amazed how you can stuff dirty laundry inside the bags without any air and make extra room for travel purchases. When you get home, it is easy to unpack the plastic bags directly to the washing machine.

93. Never take anything you can't afford to live without. It is great to travel with pictures of loved ones (take copies or download them onto your phone), but leave the family jewelry or heirlooms at home. Traveling should be light and simple, with anything irreplaceable not brought on the trip.

94. Call your cell phone carrier and ask about international plans. Most major cell phone carriers - Verizon, AT & T, T-Mobile and Sprint - offer some type of international roaming plan that you can turn off and on for the month you are traveling. Paying $5.99 a month for a reduced rate per minute is worth it on a five-minute phone call. However, for free text and talk, use Skype or What's App Messenger or Facebook Messenger. All are FREE.

95. If you have a smartphone, tablet, or iPad, understand how the free Wi-Fi works. Traveling internationally, you can use free Wi-Fi on your phone or tablet or laptop as long as you understand the Wi-Fi settings. When traveling by train in Europe from Paris to Belgium, I used free Wi-Fi on the train for two hours and checked all my email. It's a great time to work on photos.

96. Whatever type of job or career you are in, leave it behind on vacation. This is your time to relax and

not think about work. No matter who you are, the world can live without you for a week. It's good for your health and your business.

97. If you are checking luggage, take one pair of underwear and any essential must-have item you need to get ready in the morning (makeup, hairbrush, deodorant) and carry it with you. If your bag is lost or delayed, it is much easier to wear clothes again or buy a shirt than it is to find a Victoria's Secret bra size or panties in a foreign country.

98. If you're going to a beach destination, carry on a bathing suit... you can live in this for days if your luggage is lost. Pack some small sample packages of laundry detergent in your luggage. This will come in handy when the weather is not as you'd planned and you only have one or two short-sleeve shirts. Wash them out!

99. Buy a steno pad before you leave and take it with you. Better yet, find a journal type app on your phone and start a travel journal. In the morning with your coffee, or before you go to sleep, write a few journal notes. If you keep doing this on every trip, you will have a priceless journal of trips taken and memories that might otherwise be forgotten. Check out travel journal apps on your smartphone. Hot tip: try Trip Journal: it's a great way to create a travelogue of your travel experiences and share them with friends and family.

Be accepting without being judgmental and keep your eyes open and your heart full of love, and you will gain much more than a vacation.

"If you reject the food, ignore the customs, fear the religion and avoid the people, you might better stay at home." – **James Michener**

Chapter 7

Top Hottest Websites And Apps To Save You Money On Travel- *check these hot websites first, before you give your credit card number for another hotel room or airplane ticket or hit buy online*

tripadvisor.com – Trip Advisor is a free site with reviews from real people who travel. It covers almost every place imaginable. According to Trip Advisor, it has around 7 million accommodations, restaurants, and attractions. Yes, 7 million in 2017! With just under 400 million unique monthly visitors and a partnership where you can directly book hotels in the app with Trip Advisor-branded sites, it is the largest travel community in the world. The numbers speak for themselves. So, before you start planning your next trip, start with a visit to Trip Advisor. I never book a vacation without first checking the place on Trip Advisor – even if it's just to gather a second opinion.

A great way to use this site is to figure out where you want to go, look up the specific city, town or village, and peruse their "top ten" lists. Some are listed as #1 hotels because of value, others because of luxury. It is a great starting place, with free downloadable destination guides that provide detailed information in about ten pages. Categories include best places to eat, sleep, and play. The guides are updated and are current by the season. With City Destination Guides and over 170 million reviews on hotels, restaurants, and attractions, it is a great website to use to check out your hotel and the surrounding area.

Tip: when reading reviews of hotels or accommodations, please note there is always a person who writes the one negative review or who had a negative experience. Throw out the best review and the worst review and focus on the rest of the reviews. Regardless of how great a place is, unfortunately, someone had a bad experience and decided to write about it. My advice is to read a few to determine the rest of the story. In a realistic world, you can't please everyone all the time. The majority of travelers will speak the truth. Spend some time on this site: it will help you narrow down where to stay and will provide ideas of what to do on the trip. You can also sign up for Trip Advisor updates on a particular location, so when a new review comes in or a special hotel has a sale, you will receive an email. Trip Advisor also has an Android app and IPhone app.

Another cost-saving feature is that when you look at a specific hotel or resort, you can check the rate for the days you're thinking of going and it will let you compare up to 6 sites such as Expedia, Travelocity, Priceline, Venere, Orbitz and Bookit (among others), all with one search.

Airbnb-If you haven't used this fantastic marketplace for travel—what are you waiting for? Airbnb was founded in 2008 in San Francisco and since then the concept has exploded, allowing travelers to stay in unique accommodations in over 191 countries.

Never in the history of travel has there been such an eclectic database of homes to rent. Members can experience a day to day life in a farmhouse in Ireland or in a sandcastle in Mexico. Travelers can book a villa on the beach or a room in a castle online or from their phone or tablet.

If you have space to rent out, members can become hosts and can find a way monetize extra space and second homes.

Sign up to be a member of Airbnb and use this code to get $35 off your first rental: (www.airbnb.com/c/anitak103).

luxurylink.com – Luxury Link is an exciting website surf. Be warned: this site can become very addictive. User-friendly, Luxury Link offers a variety of travel packages. You have an opportunity to get a great travel package at a luxury resort for a discount. The staffers behind Luxury

Link really do their homework. Every place I have visited has not disappointed and truly represents a luxury package. If I want to narrow the nicest resorts in a destination I'm thinking of visiting, I check Luxury Link to see what places they have listed for that location. The secret of Luxury Link is that they tend to be right on picking the really cool luxury places in a destination. If it is listed on the Luxury Link site, I know it is going to be an amazing 4- or 5-star option.

Personally, this is one of my top sites, and I have used Luxury Link for many trips. Packages I have purchased resulted in a 30% to 50% savings and included extras such as airport pick-up, spa packages, and even a private romantic candlelit dinner on the beach. It is a travel package, not just a room.

For our honeymoon in St. Lucia I found a hidden gem called Ladera. This unique place has only three walls and is 1000 feet up on a cliff with a hot tub in front looking over the majestic jagged rock mountains of the Pitons and the translucent sea. Finding this unique luxury hideaway was special and it was discovered because it once had a travel package offered on Luxury Link. Even though no luxury packages existed at the time of planning our honeymoon, we contacted the resort directly. Secret tip: Mention the package on Luxury Link and see if they have any unpublished rates or packages that you could buy directly from them comparable to what they had previously offered on Luxury Link.

My great finds on Luxury link included an entire week for two in an upscale waterfront villa in Belize with many extras. Special inclusive luxuries were built in the package: besides the beautiful accommodations, a three-course private dinner, a snorkeling trip, free fly fishing lesson, and a massage - all for under $745 for the week for two (this also included the taxes)! Additionally, it included free pick up and drop off to the island airport and a boat ride to the resort. Extras really add up on vacations, so understanding the value of packages is important. The dinner would have been at least a $200 bill, the massage $100, and the snorkeling for two at least $150. Add in the water taxi ride (round trip for $40) and basically your accommodations cost less than $250 for the week.

In Costa Rica, another unique package included a Shaman and a Hogan ceremony with a volcanic mud massage at the base of the volcano at the Tabacon Hot Springs at the Arenal volcano. This ceremony is something we would probably never have thought to purchase on our own, but since it was included in the package, we experienced a unique ritual. In Playa del Carmen we scored three nights in an all-inclusive resort with an oceanfront Junior suite for a price less than the one-night room rate advertised on the resort's webpage.

Luxury Link is my go-to place for great luxury at unbelievable prices. Check it out and make sure to look at the whole package, as it generally is more than just the accommodations.

Expedia.com – Expedia is one of the largest online companies in the world. Over 90% of the trips I've booked on Expedia are lower or the same as the resort websites and other websites that tout travel deals. Expedia has a portfolio of over 150 travel apps in 70 countries and 35 languages. Their portfolio includes Hotel.com, Orbitz, Trivago, Homeaway, Travelocity, Hotwire, Venere, and Classic vacations; among others. If you are booking a trip, it will be worth your time to check Trip Advisor and then one of the Expedia companies to see what the lowest rate will be before going to the resort's website. These three checks, for those who don't have much time for research, will target your trip in a fair price category. You can feel confident that if there is a low-cost fare out there, 90% of the time you probably found it. Additionally, if you need a flight and car rental, the package deals will end up lower on Expedia. Please note: Expedia does not represent all the airlines. Southwest Airlines and a few international airlines companies are not on the site. Expedia represents the most popular US airline carriers and will let you use your frequent flyer number and earn miles on all trips at the discounted prices. Additionally, if you use the site frequently, they do send coupons for future vacations booked on Expedia. Expedia has user reviews which are helpful, and you can sort them by lowest price and star rating. You can view rooms and maps, and generally they have a liberal cancellation policy. The cancellation policy is available before you book, so you can see what your options are to change or cancel a trip. If you do not want to book online, they have a toll-free number with helpful customer service. Google the Expedia app to see if coupons or promotions exist, if you download the app.

Kayak, Bing and Yahoo – kayak.com, bing.com and Yahoo.com. Kayak, Bing and Yahoo are very similar websites. They will pull up travel information comparing multiple sites at one time. They will also allow you to use low fare finder graphs to help identify the least expensive time to travel. Hotels, airfare, and rental cars are all listed on this comparison site.

Hotwire.com and **Priceline.com** – A great site to check out car rentals, hotel rooms, airfare, and to negotiate rates. If you are a flexible traveler, you can bid on rental rates and hotel rooms in specific categories.

VRBO.com – VRBO was invented before Airbnb and is very similar; but the rentals are for the entire house. If you have not checked out this site, it is worth looking at right now. VRBO or Vacations Rental by Owner is really a great site that allows you to stay in vacation homes around the world.

You can sort by country or by state and view pictures and email the owners with questions. Because the accommodations are people's vacation homes, they offer many amenities such as fully equipped kitchens, a media library, games, or even beach chairs and beach equipment (for beach rentals). You can search by size and can even find something pet friendly. This is a great alternative for groups of all sizes, from couples to large families. You can browse through property photos, amenity lists and traveler reviews. Depending on what type of vacation you are looking for, this is worth checking out. Similar sites for vacation condos and homes owned by individuals are at www.homeaway.com, www.flipkey.com and www.vacationrentals.com.

Getaroom.com – This site is similar to hotels.com, but does two unique things. It compiles guest satisfaction survey results from Trip Advisor, AOL, Yahoo and other sites, and places a guest satisfaction survey rating beside the typical 3-, 4- or 5-star hotel rating. Its travel secret is its unpublished rate. How this works is: after you see the lowest rate online, it tells you to call the number, ask for the unpublished rate (which the hotel cannot reveal, as it is unpublished), and then if you decide to book, you will see a rate lower than the rate you saw online. The site states that 60% of hotels will do the unpublished rate, which can be anywhere from 20% or 50% off the lowest rate listed online. One issue to consider is the cancellation rate. Read before you book.

Jetsetter.com – This site offers unpublished low rates for luxury destinations. The special highly discounted deals at luxury places are only offered for a brief number of days (called a "Flash sale"). With a small number of locations and offerings, you need to check the site weekly and see if you are interested in traveling to one of the destinations of the week. You can also refer friends to the site by invitation, and if they book a night, you get $25 credit toward a unique vacation. Accommodations are top-notch in the 4- or 5-star category with rates at 25% to 60% off.

Couchsurfing.org – This is a worldwide network offering free lodging in over 120,000 different cities. Yes, *free*, in case you missed that word. On their website or phone app, Couchsurfing defines who they are: "Couchsurfing is a global community of 9 million people in more than 120,000 cities who share their life, their world, their journey. Couchsurfing connects travelers with a global network of people willing to share in profound and meaningful ways, making travel a truly social experience." This non-profit organization is Facebook meets Expedia. It is a website where travelers can register ($25 for verification), meet other travelers and get local advice, meet with a native expert, and even plan future stays. My niece and nephew used this site in Dublin, Ireland. The local resident they stayed with worked as a tour guide at the Guinness factory and went out of her way to accommodate them. When the morning alarm failed to go off, she even helped them with a taxi to the airport.

This site isn't for everyone, but it is worth checking out for meeting some fellow travelers online and gathering travel advice.

Bookingbuddy.com – Booking Buddy is like Kayak or Bing. One of its great features, which is very simple to use, is its airfare alerts. Pick your departure city and your arrival city and an estimated time frame of when you are thinking of traveling. Like magic, when fares drop you will receive an email and they will list the fares for your time frame to help you with your planning and decision-making. They can also email you fares from your city to any city when there is a special, so you can plan a spontaneous trip.

Venere.com – Great site for international traveling. Many places that are not on Expedia will be on here (even though it's owned by Expedia). You can pick your currency, and the prices are competitive. Using this for Paris and Belgium hotels gave me over 30% off from any other rate I could find online or by calling the hotel.

Bookit.com – This site has proved to be competitive and has great discounts. Just make sure that when you look at prices, you understand if it is per person or per night.

Orbitz.com, and **Travelocity.com** all offer discounted rates and travel packages. Both sites are similar to their parent travel site, Expedia, and they offer complete packages, including hotels and airfare. Traveler ratings are listed beside each discounted hotel along with star ratings. Travelzoo.com and Booking.com are additional sites worth checking out.

Groupon.com – Groupon has many travel deals. If you have not used this site for local dining or spa services, it is worth checking out. Here, services are offered at huge discounts. The catch? Read the fine print and know the expiration date or limitations. If you are planning on spending some time in a big city, check this out before you go. If you're flexible, they have some tremendous savings on hotel stays and attractions. Search Groupon's travel deals.

Travel Apps

You've heard the saying "They have an app for that." Well, travel sites are no exception. Every website listed above has a free app. There are thousands of travel apps available for your tablet or smartphone. Travel Apps on your smartphone is the secret weapon you want to take with you.

For those traveling in large cities such as London, Paris, San Francisco, or New York, numerous smartphone apps exist for bus schedules, subway routes, and even taxi assistance. Many applications offer translators, currency conversion tables, and detailed maps. There are apps for everything: go to your app store and Google what interests you.

Free travel apps for your smartphone are plentiful. Many useful low-cost apps for travel are also available, but let's focus on the free applications. Below are a few of my favorite free travel apps for your phone. Try a few out on your next vacation and you will wonder how you traveled without them.

What's app - a free app used by billions! You can have face to face conversations, text, and voice calls for FREE. Just find a wi-fi hotspot and use your smartphone. Long distance charges for texting and talking become extinct. Before you leave, make sure all your friends and family have this app set up. You'll never have to pay for international calling again.

Airline apps - If your vacation involves getting in a plane, download the airline app. Complete your account and all your future flights will show up with confirmation codes and alerts, if the trip becomes delayed. You can check in directly on your phone and don't have to scramble to find flight numbers and record locaters. You can also save your electronic boarding pass.

Kayak, Trip Advisor, Expedia, Hotel tonight – If you find yourself on vacation and you want to extend your trip, no need to worry - if you have your smartphone, you can still book the best online deals available. With just one click on any of the above travel apps, you can check a variety of websites and compare prices for car, hotel, and airfare. Yes, you can book the room on your smartphone without a computer.

Weatherchannel – This free app is always on my phone so I can check the weather of my current location and where I am traveling to. Accuweather and Weatherbug are free apps that do the same thing.

Aroundme – The name speaks for itself. You're traveling in an unknown city, you open the app, and like magic you know what's around you. Banks, bars, coffee shops, gas stations, hospitals - you name it; they list what's around you. Who knew that cozy Italian restaurant with delicious bruschetta was located on the small street behind you?

Urbanspoon – If you are on your urban vacation or are exploring the closest city to you, check out this app which will give you great restaurants with reviews. Yelp is similar and can assist in the same manner. Foodspotting.com also helps find the best food.

WiFiFinder – Get connected. This is a great application for finding Wi-Fi hotspots when traveling; especially when traveling overseas when you need to do a little travel work. The site does show both free and paid Wi-Fi spots.

Skype – Skype is a great app to help with international calling. Use the above app (**Wi-Fi finder**) to find a hot spot and call your friends and family on Skype for free. Free phone calls from your tropical island in the South Pacific - now that's a smart vacation.

HearPlanet(lite)- Featured as "the world's largest audio guide," this is for travelers who like to create their own tours and have their guidebook speak to them. You'll get the scoop on nearby attractions, landmarks, and the history behind them; all in the palm of your hand. (One word of advice: make sure you have an external battery charger. This app can wear down your battery as it notifies you in real time of cool sights to see.)

Sitorsquat – If you belong to the Small Bladder Club, like I do, then this is the application for you (it's very helpful with small children or for pregnant women). It is one of the first inventories of bathroom listings. International listings are not as plentiful as US listings, but this app continues to be updated.

Googlemaps – Hopefully everyone who has a smartphone has used this application for directions, finding what's near regarding restaurants, shopping, or even gas stations. This is one app I cannot live without. You can also type in your airline and flight number, and it will provide an update on flight status.

Google skymaps – If you haven't looked at this application, you're missing out. On your vacation, you have time to relax and look at the stars. This will give you your sky map, tell you where stars and planets are in the night sky, and will show you the constellations. Simply amazing technology.

Flighttracker – Yes, this app will track your flights and help you with any unforeseen delays. Airlines have apps of their own, so if you are a frequent flyer, check out your airline and download that app. Check out a similar app, Trip-It.

Freetranslator – Depending on where you're visiting, check out the free translators for various languages. You never know when you will need it, so download your vacation country ahead of time and it may help you out in the most serious of situations. Check out a similar app, Google Translator.

Currencyconverter – This is a simple currency converter and exchange rate calculator. When you're on the go, this can come in handy, and you can set your preferences.

The websites and smartphone apps listed above are no-fee websites and apps. Many websites offer toll-free phone numbers for assistance in case you want to call and not book online. But, if you don't have a smartphone, it might be time for you to invest in one. What it can save you in travel and guidance is well worth the cost. Free calling, texting, and maps are essential when traveling; and with a smartphone, all you have to do is find wi-fi.

Hot tip#1: Clear your web browser, if you are using the same computer for different searches. I have witnessed two different airline prices on two different computers.

Hot Tip #2: Yes, smartphones are essential when traveling; but it is good to unplug when you have reached your destination, even if it's only for a little while.

"A journey is like marriage. The certain way to be wrong is to think you control it." – **John Steinbeck**

Chapter 8

Secrets To Making Your Next Trip, A Trip Of A Lifetime — *all vacations can be trips of a lifetime: a little planning and research will make every trip its own unique memory*

So, what is the secret to making your next vacation a "trip of a lifetime"? Well, unfortunately there is not just **one** magic secret or **one** simple quick tip that will insure that every vacation for the rest of your life is a "trip of a lifetime." With a few secret insider tips and some thoughtful planning, each and every vacation can become a lifetime memory that you will find unique and meaningful. With a little effort and time, your journey will be special, you can create a memory, and you will have a trip of a lifetime.

Secret #1 – **Get excited!** Before you go, print out a few pictures from a website, brochure or magazine and hang them on your refrigerator, computer, or bulletin board.

Even your bathroom mirror will work! When you wake up... bang! Your vacation picture is right in front of you, helping you start the day off with good thoughts and excitement about the trip to come. Excitement is good for the soul. Get enthusiastic, talk about it, and hang a picture. Try it: what do you have to lose?

Secret #2 – If you have the time, do a little research ahead of time and find something atypical at or near your destination. **Plan one unusual activity** for your upcoming trip - something that takes you out of your box. Think outside the box. This is your vacation - do something new or unusual. Researching it ahead of time and planning at least one extraordinary event will help set this trip apart from trips in the past. Caving? Zip-lining? Cooking class? Drum-making class? Snowshoeing? Dogsled riding? Tequila tasting? The list goes on. Do something epic on your vacation.

Secret #3 – Learn more about the destination. Rent a movie or order a book that is set in the destination you are visiting. Search for the city or country on line. For example: going to Puerto Vallarta? Type in, *what movies or books are filmed in Puerto Vallarta?* An old classic may come up, such as Night of the Iguana with Ava Gardner and Richard Burton. Never heard of it? Neither did I. But, I watched the film and then found the location of the house along the beach, and have some remarkable photos to prove it. Try to retrace the steps of the characters and see the journey from a different point of view. Fiction or nonfiction, if the story takes place in the setting you are visiting, it will be based on historical places you might want to visit.

Secret #4 – Volunteer or participate in some type of community service in the city, town, or village you are visiting. Email your resort, hotel or lodging and ask if they know of any organization that may need a volunteer for the day. You may be astonished at what you will gain by giving one day of your vacation to someone in need. The memories of giving back will indeed make it a trip of a lifetime. The resort may not be used to this request, but do it anyway; you will end up meeting local folks and perhaps starting a new trend. Email me for assistance, or go to www.wordstravelfilm.com - I would love to help.

Secret #5 – Listen to local music from your destination. Go to the local library or go to ITunes or buy a CD online that comes from the area you are visiting. It can be as simple as Appalachian music if you're visiting the Appalachians, or Belizean music from Belize. Just Google the name of the destination and the word "music," and you will find many unexpected choices. Most libraries have an online system where you can place a hold request for specific music. The library will even email you when it's ready for pick up.

Secret #6 – Invite a family member, or someone who needs an excuse for getting away from it all, to go on your trip with you. Share the tips you have learned in this book on saving money for the trip and ask them to help research, save, and plan. These trips will make a memory that will stay in your heart for a lifetime. You may also be helping someone take a vacation, who really needs one. Better yet, buy this book for that person in your life who really needs a vacation. Inspire them.

Secret #7 – Make a memory book, scrapbook, photo book, or online video when you return. Everyone takes pictures. When you come back, make sure you download your pictures, take them to a store with a photo department, and order your photos in an album or look at all the online deals for photobooks (some as cheap as 5.99 or less). You can be creative and do this on your computer with an option to pick them up at the nearest Wal-Mart, Costco, Walgreens or other outlet, through an online provider. Online sites such as <u>Walgreens</u> or <u>www.mypublisher.com</u> will mail you the books once you drop your photos in their easy-to-use form. The books will help preserve the memories of your trip for a lifetime.

Remember what the definition of a vacation is? It doesn't have to be the trip to Bora Bora or Australia to qualify as a trip of a lifetime. The journey, the memories, and the time you share with others, coupled with the relaxation, trying something new, getting out of your routine – these make a vacation a "trip of a lifetime".

Whatever it is that you love doing with your free time, do it on your vacation and live in that moment. Let everything else sit on the desk for a while.

"He who does not travel does not know the value of men."– Moorish proverb

Chapter 9

10 Ways to GO GREEN, *and Save Enough Money For A Vacation*

GO GREEN – Ten years ago, the majority of folks would not even know what the statement "Go Green" means. Now it has become part of our vocabulary; part of billion dollar companies' tag lines. Today, unless you have been locked in a trailer watching old video games, you know what the term "Going Green" means and are hopefully trying to incorporate a green way of life into your everyday habits.

Go Green, Eco-Friendly, and Carbon Footprint are part of our vocabulary. We hear these terms--but do we understand them? Saving our planet is the single most important crisis we will face in our lifetime. But, it's a crisis we may not believe or understand until years down the road.

So, what does this have to do with travel? Everything. We explore and we travel to open our hearts and our minds; to experience this magnificent living planet. If we want the beauty of this world to continue not just for us but for generations to come, for the children and grandchildren who aren't even born yet, we must educate ourselves.

Easy alternatives exist when it comes to energy consumption. If every citizen participated in 'going green', we would have endless travel days left.

Movies have jumped into the action of educating about the environment, using film to portray what may happen if we keep living the way we are behaving. Even animated films (Finding Nemo or Wall-e) portray the peril the world faces if we don't wake up. Films such as the Oscar award-winning *Avatar* can help educate the leaders of tomorrow's world by showing them what may happen in the future if we don't start changing, and series shows such as The Walking Dead can scare the you-know-what out of us. Are we listening?

Ten years from now, if you are not going green in your everyday living, I believe you will be penalized in some form; though I am not quite sure how that will be implemented - maybe through taxes of some kind, such as paying a higher tax on non-green items. Implementing rebates for buying new, energy-efficient appliances and solar energy sources is a great idea. If you need to replace something, why not make it affordable to replace it with something more green. The truth of the matter is, if we want to keep the world around us safe and make it a better place for the future, we are all going to have to jump on the recycle, re-use wagon.

In today's world there are advocates and thousands of ideas about saving our planet and going green. There are websites, books, films, and even television channels that provide information. There are those who some may call "extreme advocates" because they will only live in a green manner. Ed Begley Jr. has been going green since the 1970s. He rides his bike to make toast, lives 98% off the grid, and is the author of several books on the subject. Featured in the Discovery Channel show *Living with Ed* on Planet Green, he, among others, shows how Tiny Houses and Off the Grid choices are role models for green living. Going green and getting the basics down is easier than we think.

Some ideas you may have read about to reduce our carbon footprint sound a little extreme . There are ways to reduce the carbon footprint without eliminating travel.

With technology changing and going in the "save the planet" direction, new ideas are evolving daily and will assist everyday consumers with easy ways to go green.

The good news is that learning how to go green - even knowing just the basics - will help the planet. If you implement the ideas below, you will save enough money to take an extra vacation this year. Now, that's my kind of good news.

Here are some top energy-saving tips on basic ways to go green this year and save money for a vacation.

- Set your thermostat a few degrees lower in the winter and a few degrees higher in the summer, to save on heating and cooling costs. Do you have a programmable thermostat? If not, get one – it will instantly save you money.
- Change your curtains for the season. Heavy curtains in winter will help keep the room warm. White curtains, as well as solar shades and screens, can reflect heat for sunny days.
- Get rid of the old light bulbs! Install compact fluorescent light bulbs (CFLs) or LEDs when your older incandescent bulbs burn out. Amazon has them cheaper than ever.
- Unplug appliances when you're not using them. Or, use a "smart" power strip that senses when appliances are off and cuts "phantom" or "vampire" energy use. Televisions, DVDs, and computers still use power, even if they are turned off. You can save additional money every month by using power strips and switching everything off when you leave the house. Try it out for one cycle of your bill and count the money that will be going towards a vacation, on your next bill.
- Wash clothes in cold water. Seriously: if you're not doing this, you're wasting money. Almost 85 percent of energy used to machine wash clothes goes towards heating the water.
- Turn your hot water heater down by at least 20 degrees. Is it above 120 degrees? Go check it. Lower it; you will save money monthly that can go towards vacation dollars.
- Go through your closet. Schedule this job in your calendar. Try to pare down to one hundred items of clothing. Tell yourself, *I can*

keep one hundred things... then sell the rest to the consignment shop and put the money away in your travel savings fund. Okay, if you can't do one hundred (I can't!), just start the process of trying to get to one hundred and gather at least two or three bags.

- Think about every purchase you make, this year. If you buy new clothes, get rid of something old: donate it and use the tax write off, or consign it.
- Use a drying rack or clothesline to save energy on drying your clothes. Have you ever smelled hang-dried sheets? They smell fresh. Many of your clothes will last longer and stay in better shape without hot dryers.
- Buy a travel mug and use it when you get coffee or soda to go. If we all used one less paper cup, imagine how many trees we would save and how we would make less trash for landfills. Yes, refills are cheaper. Add this to your travel money fund; it all adds up.
- Fill up your freezer. Believe it or not, this will make your freezer more energy efficient, saving you money. Ice counts!
- Fix leaky faucets and toilets. Water drips cost money every month - make sure they are fully stopped and that your house is leak free.
- Buy aerators (small circle screens) and put them in your faucets. They are very inexpensive and will save one to two gallons of water per minute, and not noticeably affect your water pressure.

- Check the year of your toilets. Toilets from 1970 to 1980 take significantly more gallons of water to flush. It may be more efficient to install newer toilets.
- Use energy-efficient dishwashers instead of hand washing. A water-smart dishwasher uses 6 to 10 gallons per cycle, while hand washing can use over 20 gallons per sink load.
- Check out www.skoy.com. One Skoy dishcloth replaces 17 rolls of paper towels. Starting at $5-6 per package, the money saving over a year will add up for a huge vacation savings.
- Make sure all your doors and windows are insulated in winter and summer to ensure that air coming in costs less to heat or cool down. Use caulk, weather stripping, or even plastic film kits to create insulation. This will save you money.
- Try a month of not buying bottled water. Use a Brita water pitcher or other water filtration unit of your choice. Go to www.Brita.com or just research water filtration systems. Note how much you save in a month and multiply by twelve.
- Take your lunch to work. Use a lunch box with reusable containers instead of paper and plastic. Eating in will save you money, and bringing home the containers will help save the environment.
- Think about transportation. This is a very basic way to start to go green and can save you money and improve your health. Can you cut down on your monthly gas bill and help the environment? Bike, walk, or car pool. Check out the public transportation and try this even

if it is just once a month. You can save money on gas and on parking and have time to read a book or check your emails on the bus. If you know you need to go to an area for shopping, plan out your trip so that instead of driving to the store ten times in a week, cut down to one trip a week.

o   Think about the saying "use, reuse, reduce and recycle."

Okay, do you think you will have enough money to go on a vacation by implementing some of the above strategies for going green? Let's add up some potential savings from using just a few of the energy saving tips above.

1. Turning down the hot water heater can shave $10 to $ 20 a month off your electric bill. Potential travel money = $240 a year.

2. Changing half your lights to energy-efficient light bulbs saves $100- $200 a year.

3. Putting all your plugged-in appliances on energy strips and turning all power off when you leave: depending on your house and the items you always leave on, this tactic could be significant. Try this for one month and see the difference. We will be conservative and say that the figure will be $20 a month, resulting in $240 of extra vacation money for the year.

4. Using www.skoy.com cloths instead of paper towels for a year will save at least $200-$300 a year.

5. Cleaning out your closet and selling to a consignment store - let's be conservative = $200 for the travel budget.

6. Using a travel mug to buy refill coffee five days a week will save $240 a year.

7. Walk, ride or share. Biking, walking, public transportation or carpooling, even twice a week, can result in huge savings in your pocket and will reduce your carbon footprint. Keep this in mind when traveling: using public transportation is a great way to understand the local people. Doing so twice a week can result in saving $10 a week, depending on the distance, resulting in a conservative guess of $500 a year.

8. Eat less meat. Yes, according to a report by The United Nations' Food and Agriculture Organization, they estimate that the meat industry generates nearly one-fifth of man-made greenhouse gas emission - more than the entire transportation sector. Meat consumption has accelerated over the last 50 years, and if everyone tried to reduce their meat intake, we could reduce our carbon footprint. And guess what? Meat is more expensive than vegetables, pasta, or beans. Pack on the savings: have a meatless Monday. The potential travel money is $10 a week, resulting in $520 a year.

9. Taking your lunch to work. Even if you do this one or two times a week, you'll save at least $10 a week. Estimate: $500 a year.

10. Plant a tree - go to the Arbor Day Foundation and join for ten dollars, and receive ten free trees. Plant a tree in an unshaded area of your house to reduce your bill. Trees help stop climate change by removing carbon dioxide from the air and they release oxygen. Trees help urban pollution. Shade can reduce your cooling bill by at least 5%. The potential travel money = $120 a year (plus free trees).

Being very conservative, if you tried the above green tips for one year, you will have saved somewhere in the ballpark of $2000-$4000 for the year.

Using the travel secrets in this book, $2000 is a great travel budget for the year. Simple, but yet it takes effort. So, before you think "I want to vacation, but I don't have the money!", think about the travel tips in this chapter. Go ahead: try some out and put the money away for a vacation. It's free money that takes little planning and results in a greener world and more fabulous vacations.

To determine your carbon footprint and learn other energy-saving tips, go to www.nature.org (carbon calculator) and www.earthday.org .

"To my mind, the greatest reward and luxury of travel is to be able to experience everyday things as if for the first time, to be in a position in which almost nothing is so familiar it is taken for granted." – Bill Bryson

Chapter 10

Ten Trips You Can Take All For A Tank Of Gas...

Pack a lunch from home, make some homemade sweet tea or a big thermos of Kool-Aid, and take a vacation for the cost of a tank of gas...

Okay, I know what you're thinking ... vacation near home? Doesn't sound like fun. In fact, you might not even read this last chapter because you have learned multiple new ways to save money for travel. You found some tips on how to go green in the previous chapter, and will save vacation money for next year. You are now ready to spend some time online and peruse the suggested websites to get started on vacation planning. You get that. It makes sense. How can ten trips that you can take for a tank of gas be a vacation? Let's stop for a minute to think about where you live. Well, do a little more than think: how about visualizing it. Need a little help? Pull up a map of your location and surrounding area, from your computer. Go to a local visitors tourism stand and pick up a free map of the area, stop at the local chamber of commerce, or look at the driving atlas at your local AAA office. Get a map, make a mark where you live, and then look at the little key on the bottom of the map. Figure out what 200–300 miles would be in any direction - take a paper plate, a compass, a Frisbee, or whatever is round in your house and draw a circle around your hometown.

Depending on what type of energy-efficient or gas guzzling vehicle you own, your vehicle will get at least 20–40 miles to a gallon. Most likely you have at least a 10-20-gallon tank (I hope so). Take a moment to calculate how far you can go on a tank of gas. Take a close look at the circle. Have you been everywhere in that area? Look at the markings on the map. What do you see as far as geographical and historical symbols that mark points of interest?

I know, I know ... you live so close to all this; is this really a vacation? Well, stop and think about it for a moment. Wherever you live in this great big world of ours, in any given 200–300-mile radius around you, someone is traveling for some type of vacation.

Yes, there could be exceptions, if you live 300 miles from anything. There are very few large bodies of land, however, that do not have visitors. My friend once lived in a small fishing lodge in Alaska and, yes, 300 miles from civilization. Folks did come up there seasonally, to fish or hike or explore. Someone in this world is going on vacation to see something **near you** or in your radius.

Whether it be a historical marker of the civil war, a natural cave, or a unique hiking spot, someone is traveling from far away to visit your area. Rural areas contain many historical or nature adventures. Cities offer a plethora of events and unknown places to visit. Suburban areas might have outlet shopping or cool outdoor spaces for a sports event.

I once heard of a study about people who lived near Walt Disney World but never visited the famous amusement park. I can't remember the exact percentage, but I do remember it was an astonishing statistic, in the ballpark of something like three out of four people who live near Disney World never entered the magical world of Disney. Disney World in Florida reported in 2015 that they had attendance of over 40 million visitors annually. Think about that number. 40 million visitors from all over the globe travel to visit this location, yet many who live within driving distance have never made it a priority. Quite amazing.

This 'live close, but don't go' mentality is a common occurrence with many popular tourist spots. A large number of people who live near sites like Niagara Falls, the Grand Canyon, the Statue of Liberty, or even the Eiffel Tower have never vacationed at these tourist destination spots right next door. What big tourist destination is in your radius that you have never seen or taken your children or family to see? Why not? Is it because it is too close?

Living in Arizona, I know many friends, relatives, and co-workers who live here but have never witnessed the great vastness and stunning natural beauty of the Grand Canyon. Maybe they are afraid of getting sucked in by the sheer vertical force and energy of the Grand Canyon; or perhaps in their mind a trip to a location in their vicinity doesn't count as a vacation. Why not?

It's not just the most famous of landmarks nearby that residents don't experience. If folks live near Disney World and don't take the time to go visit, imagine the small, lesser known attractions or natural wonders next door. Does an attraction somehow become less interesting when it is close by?

Ask any friend or relative who works in a city near the beach how many times they physically go and walk on the beach? The answers might scare you. People from all over the world travel to these famous or unique beach destinations, while others live their whole lives without going around the corner.

So, change your current mindset. The only difference between tourists and you, right now, is **they** have to buy an airline ticket, train passage, or drive across country to get there. Camping or booking a night in a motel or hotel is required, as well. You, on the other hand, just need to set your alarm, wake up in the morning, and take a drive from your house.

Every locale is someone's next vacation destination.

Sometimes you need to get out of your comfort zone and try new things. If you take risks and try something a little different, in your radius, you may be surprised. Maybe you're the world traveler who goes everywhere else in the world and loves exotic destinations. Well, start at home. Go to new restaurants you have never tried, or sample different ethnic foods in your area. Look at your surroundings with a new sense of wonder ... you may discover unknown destination vacations right in your own backyard.

If you are low on money this year, take a "stay vacation." Big resort areas coined this phrase "stay vacation" in the hotel business due to low hotel occupancy and economic recession. It was a successful campaign where local folks enjoyed special deals for family vacations and luxury romance vacations. Take a night out in your hometown. You may never think to check the prices or local incentives because this doesn't seem like a vacation to you. Well, we defined the word "vacation" and "travel" in the beginning of this book. Even a "stayvacation" fits the definition of vacation: "a period of time devoted to rest, travel, or recreation," as defined by Encarta Dictionary. If it is a vacation for those visiting from faraway places, why isn't it for you? You have the advantage when checking out great local deals, spending less money on travel and enjoying shorter travel times.

Stay vacations are an alternative that can help you get the vacation release you need at a much lower cost and shorter time frame, especially if you are short on vacation days. Throw in the added benefit of learning something new about your hometown or state, and taking a vacation closer to home makes sense. If you're shaking your head right now, have you ever tried it? People are traveling from all over the world to see what's in *your* backyard. Maybe you should check it out...

Depending on whether you live in the city or the country, there are scores of choices.

Here are ten trip ideas you can take, all on a tank of gas:

1. **Take notice of a State Park.** If you live in the United States, check out the State Parks near you. Try www.nps.gov. This website showcases over 400 places in the United States that fall under the umbrella of a state park. Do the math. With only 50 states and 400 places, there is bound to be a state park near you in your 200–300-mile radius. According to the website, these 400 areas see more than 275 million visitors each year. The site offers a clickable US map; click on your state and check out what is nearby. Developed by the National Park Service and the US Department of the Interior, this is a great start for planning your vacation and takes advantage of a national service created for everyone's enjoyment. Typically, you will find hiking trails or historical markers or even free events offered to the public. Check it out and you probably will be surprised at what is so close and new to you. The National Parks and Federal Recreational Lands Pass is a great savings and is good for four people. This $80 pass works at over 2,000 federal recreation sites. Each pass covers entrance fees at national parks and national wildlife refuges. Tip: Check nps.gov for National Free Park Days on holidays.

2. **Pack an old-fashioned picnic and pick a nearby destination you haven't visited in a long time - or have never visited.** Hooray for you if you have actually packed a picnic basket. When did the nostalgic, romantic, old-fashioned picnic outing disappear? Mapquest or look at your paper map and figure out the road less traveled to get there and back. Create a special moment. Think ahead and build some delicious homemade sandwiches (nice and thick, loaded with meat/veggies and cheese,) and tasty snacks, bring some cloth napkins, a picnic basket if you have one (if not, a cooler or even a suitcase will do the trick), and bring a musical instrument or a music player and a big. comfortable blanket. Don't tell the others traveling with you where they are going or what you are bringing; just tell them to take the day off for a vacation day and bring some comfortable outdoor clothes. Surprises create an unforgettable event. Don't forget the sunscreen, hats, and bug spray (just in case), and always bring lots of water. If you live in a city, look up city parks you have never visited, or sit on a bench in front of a beautiful cathedral with a small sitting area to gaze at the architecture. If country roads are in your radius or not too far away, discover a beautiful setting near a babbling creek, river, or lake. Look at the map and search out nearby bodies of water. There is bound to be a place that will help you escape from it all.

Look up the history of the location and bring that with you so you can educate yourself on what happened in that spot 100, 200, or even 500 years ago. Get out of your comfort zone and surprise someone with a delightful picnic. A little local knowledge, found with a push of a button on the computer, will make the trip even more memorable.

3. **Visit a historical marker.** With over 30,314 historical markers in the United States, I doubt if you have seen 50% of them. If you are a US resident, certainly there are several historical markers in your radius. Go to www.historicalmarkers.com and check out what is in your circle. Quoting from the top of the historical marker website, "History teaches everything including the future" by Lamartine, this is certainly an opportunity to take a "stay vacation" and gain historical insight by visiting what is near your own backyard. People travel all over the world to see such historical markers. Once again, keep in mind how lucky you are to be able to see this by traveling on a tank of gas and, at the end of the day, sleeping in your own comfortable bed.

4. **Have a go at a Museum.** If you're not a museum person, visit one anyway. We tend to visit more museums when we travel and miss the ones in our own home town. In Phoenix, AZ there is a musical instrument museum called MIM. People come from all over the globe to see this new museum and I live ten miles away and didn't even know it'd opened. Check out city vacations and visit local museums for a weekend to learn about close urban sites in your radius. Go to www.museumlink.com and click on

your state. You might be surprised at the museums that are only a tank of gas away.

5. **Seek Natural wonders and monuments.** Do you know the natural wonders of the world (or even in the United States, which are spread out across this land and worth seeing in your lifetime)? Check it out and see what is near you. Go to www.usa.org/travel/naturalwonders or sevennaturalwonders.org.

6. **Undertake a Hiking vacation.** Covering the majority of the United States, a volunteer hiking vacation can be adventurous, close by, and no cost. Go to https://volunteervacations.americanhiking.org. They have a map of the United States showing all the participating states. Their motto from their website reads, "Our nation's trails need your help! Join the American Hiking Society for a week of building and maintaining trails in exciting and diverse locations across the country. Bring only your camping gear and a willingness to get dirty. We provide the rest."

7. **Find nearby water sources.** Bodies of water go by countless names. Check out lakes, ponds, rivers, creeks, dams, streams, or waterfalls in your radius. Go swimming, fishing, kayaking, or boating. Get in the water, look at it, or sit by a beach for a day. How close is the largest body of water near you? Is it near the ocean, a sea, or a bay? Check it out and have a water day.

8. **Uncover Haunted places.** Some folks travel all over the world to see scary or eerie places. From renowned Alcatraz to the Stanley Hotel in Colorado where the movie *The Shining* was filmed to ghosts trekking through the farm fields at Gettysburg, almost every town or city has their ghost stories. A haunted site is not hard to locate, especially at Halloween. Local newspapers and websites will usually run a story or two of local haunts. Find out what is haunted, in your radius, and plan on a Fall Halloween weekend vacation to a local haunted spot. A great website to get you started is www.hauntedplacesinamerica.com.

9. **Holiday at an Amusement Park.** The internet will amaze you with all the information that is available at a push of a button. Go to www.themeparksonline.org for a list and directory of over 200 theme parks and ways to purchase advance tickets. Another good site is www.mytravelguide.com. Type in "amusement parks" – they list over 385 parks in the United States and have a listing of over 25,000 cities. For worldwide amusement parks, go to www.123world.com/amusement .

10. **Go Camping.** Investigate outdoor spaces. There are many locations in your radius where you can spend the night in a tent or explore camp-like accommodations. There are bound to be numerous places that offer camping services, both government

and non-government, nearby. Go to http://recreation.usgs.gov/camping.html for information on United States camping areas. There you will find state-specific information and ideas, and a list of the Top 100 Family Campgrounds in the United States. Another established camping resource is KOA. KOA has been around for over 50 years, offering online booking for over 450 campsites in North America. KOA offers more than just camping sites. Check out their website www.KOA.com and look at the lodges, cabins, cottages, RV sites, and unique accommodations being offered. Throughout the country they offer more than just a place to throw a tent, but also unique stays in airstreams, tree houses, and tepees. Check out the ones closest to you.

The possibilities are endless for trips that can be taken on a tank of gas. Look at local websites for cities near you, in your radius. Local contributing writers are eager to write a quick article on an upcoming event or a trip they recently experienced. With all the wonderful technology at our fingertips, even when we are in the woods, finding out local information has never been so easy. Accessible information on off-the-beaten track locales is mind-boggling. Everyone has an opinion, travel review, or blog. Connecting with local experts or consumers is as simple as an app on your phone.

Have a question about how far something is? Use social media. Ask. Someone is waiting to provide local expert advice. Check out websites that feature local travel. Type in the name of the town you are visiting, and research things to do - with a little bit of technology, you may discover a whole new world; all on a tank of gas.

With 52 weekends in a year and plenty of trips and vacations to take on one tank of gas, what are you waiting for? igure out how many vacations you are going to take this year, write them down on the next page or in your new travel journal, and plan.

Go travel, take a vacation, and explore the playground of life. Take recess as much as possible. Life's just more fun with recess and vacations, no matter how long or short they are.

Use the next page to help get started. Go ahead: start your planning, while it's fresh in your mind. Writing things down will help you. Use the notebook you purchased at the dollar store or the app on your phone/tablet or computer. The Evernote app (free) will let you start a folder for all of your travel ideas. You can keep articles, ideas, photos and label it "Weekend Vacations I Will Take This Year." Commit to a weekend getaway each month - a vacation you might be able to take on a tank of gas.

January
_____

February

March

April

May

June

July

August

September

October _____

November _____

December _____

Wait! It's not the end of the book. If you've read this far, don't stop. Do your homework. Get your notebook or app and make a list of the vacations you are going to take this year, other than weekend trips.

This year's possible vacation ideas:

Where to?

When?

Now, spend some time to write down your travel bucket list. Don't worry if you're uncertain. This list can change, be added to, crossed out, and reinvented. It's your list. You can watch it grow over the course of your lifetime. Take thirty minutes to do this for yourself, and keep this notebook (<u>again, dollar</u> store sells notebooks, so you have no excuse). Keep this travel bucket list in a prominent position. Yes, that means finding a Sharpie and writing the words "My Travel Bucket List" on the front of the notebook. Keep it by your computer or on a shelf in your bathroom - someplace you glance at every week. It's important to remind yourself where you want to go in this lifetime. If you can imagine it, it can happen. This lifetime is already in progress, so don't put it off for **some**day ... See the world, travel the lands, and experience vacations no matter how big or small.

You're worth it! Unfortunately, the fact is, you may wait to take vacations and get life started, but life doesn't wait for you.

Travel bucket list (in your lifetime, where in the world do you want to visit before you kick the bucket?):

1._____

2._____

3. _____

4. _____

5._____

6. _____

7. _____

8._____

9._____

10._____

Congratulations - you started traveling already, in your mind! Now, keep it going and take vacations using the secrets in this book. Your life will thank you for it!

"The journey not the arrival matters." – T. S. Eliot

ABOUT THE AUTHOR

Anita Kaltenbaugh is a traveler with over 100 published travel articles. Currently working on a new travel book *Chasing Continents: A Travel Bucket List For Your Life*, her motivation is to touch every continent on earth and encourage others to open their hearts and minds to the diversity of this world. She has lived in Europe, Mexico, and the United States, spending her free time traveling the world with her husband. She divides her time between Phoenix, Arizona, and the mile-high historical city, Prescott, Arizona and a wonderful little beach town named Puerto Penasco on the beautiful Sea of Cortez in Mexico. She also writes contemporary fiction under the pen name, A. K. Smith. Check out her new release, A Deep Thing by A. K. Smith on Amazon. Subscribe to her blog for updates and travel articles on off the beaten path destinations.

http://www.wordstravelfilm.com

Made in the USA
Columbia, SC
03 March 2019